Quality Issues in ICT-based Higher Education

Higher education institutions are becoming increasingly reliant upon information and communications technology (ICT) as a way of providing enhanced learning and teaching – whether this means supplementing face-to-face teaching or providing fully-fledged e-learning courses.

Lecturers in higher education are adopting new methods of working and ways of teaching using ICT, but these changes must be accompanied by a commitment to the quality and integrity of education.

This book provides a wide-ranging account of the quality issues surrounding the use of ICT in higher education, as well as developing useful advice and guidance on key areas including:

- devising an institution-wide strategy
- developing course materials
- providing distance and e-learning courses
- using ICT-assisted assessment
- adopting professional support processes.

With authoritative and practical contributions from leading experts in the field, this book will be a valuable addition to the shelves of all those involved in using ICT in higher education – managers, lecturers or education developers.

Stephen Fallows is Reader and Research Coordinator at the Centre for Exercise and Nutrition Science at University College Chester, UK. He has extensive experience of using ICT in supporting student learning with students in many countries around the world. He is, with Rakesh Bhanot, the co-editor of *Educational Development Through Information and Communications Technology* (also in the SEDA series).

Rakesh Bhanot is a Senior Lecturer in the Centre for Higher Education Development at Coventry University and has published extensively on learning and teaching issues in adult, further and higher education.

The Staff and Educational Development Series
Series Editor: James Wisdom

SEDA is the Staff and Educational Development Association. It supports and encourages developments in teaching and learning in higher education through a variety of methods: publications, conferences, networking, journals, regional meetings and research – and through various SEDA Accreditation Schemes.

SEDA
Selly Wick House
59–61 Selly Wick Road
Selly Park
Birmingham B29 7JE
Tel: 0121-415 6801
Fax: 0121-415 6802
E-mail: office@seda.ac.uk
Website: www.seda.ac.uk

Quality Issues in ICT-based Higher Education

Edited by Stephen Fallows and Rakesh Bhanot

RoutledgeFalmer
Taylor & Francis Group

LONDON AND NEW YORK

SEDA
STAFF AND EDUCATIONAL
DEVELOPMENT ASSOCIATION

First published 2005
by RoutledgeFalmer
2 Park Square, Milton Park, Abingdon, Oxon OX14 4RN

Simultaneously published in the USA and Canada
by RoutledgeFalmer
270 Madison Ave, New York, NY 10016

RoutledgeFalmer is an imprint of the Taylor and Francis Group

© 2005 Stephen Fallows, Rakesh Bhanot and Individual Contributors

Typeset in Baskerville by
Keystroke, Jacaranda Lodge, Wolverhampton
Printed and bound in Great Britain by
MPG Books Ltd, Bodmin

British Library Cataloguing in Publication Data
A catalogue record for this book is available from the British Library

Library of Congress Cataloging in Publication Data
A catalog record for this book has been requested

ISBN 0–415–33520–5 (hbk)
ISBN 0–415–33521–3 (pbk)

Contents

Notes on the editors and contributors

Peggy Bates is Reference Librarian at Kimbel Library, Coastal Carolina University in South Carolina, USA. While actively involved in reference and library instruction, she is also the Government Documents Librarian and Head of the Circulation Department. She has a BS in Business Management and an MS in Library and Information Science from the University of South Carolina. Her professional interests centre on library–patron interactions with technology-based resources and the ensuing implications for library practices.

Liz Beaty is Director (Teaching and Learning) for the Higher Education Funding Council for England (HEFCE). Liz has a Ph.D. from Surrey University and conducted research into student learning at the Open University. She worked in educational and management development at Newcastle Polytechnic, the University of Brighton and Coventry University. She ran the teacher accreditation scheme for the UK Staff and Educational Development Association (SEDA), and was SEDA co-chair from 1996 to 2000. Her publications span students' experiences of higher education, experiential and action learning, and strategies for educational change.

Rakesh Bhanot is Senior Lecturer in the Centre for Higher Education Development at Coventry University. He has worked in several European countries, and has delivered seminars and workshops on a variety of educational topics in many parts of the world. Prior to his current post, Rakesh was the European Co-ordinator and Programme Manager for Public Broadcasting for Multicultural Europe (PBME) – a pan-European organisation of which he was a co-founder. He has also worked in the adult and further education sector and was a national project officer with the Further Education Unit. He considers himself to be a reformed 'technophobe'.

Nicholas Bowskill is Open and Flexible Learning Adviser in the Staff Development Unit at Sheffield University. Previously, he was a research associate on the Computer Based Collaborative Group Work Project. He is also a tutor on the M.Ed. course in Networked Collaborative Learning in the School of Education. He has been involved in professional development and learning technology for ten years and has worked in different higher education institutions using open learning, face-to-face and networked strategies to support academic staff.

Adrian Bromage currently works at Coventry University's Centre for Higher Education Development, where he is currently involved in two major research projects, the evaluation of the University's 'Learn Online' initiative and the ESERC-funded ETL project. His first degree is in psychology, he has two Masters degrees in ergonomics and cognitive science, and has recently completed a doctoral thesis which explores academics' perceptions of and attitudes towards technology-led change.

Glynis Cousin is Academic Development Adviser at the Centre for Academic Practice, Warwick University where she carries out research and development activities to support research-based learning. She is also Associate Director for an Edinburgh University-led national research project into the enhancement of teaching and learning in undergraduate education.

Frances Deepwell is a Fellow of SEDA (Staff and Educational Development Association). Currently, her work portfolio includes maintaining the institution-wide delivery of WebCT and providing support to academic colleagues across Coventry University. Originally a translator, she entered higher education to develop innovative ways of teaching translation. Over the past twelve years, she has developed expertise in the use of a variety of technologies and their practical application in learning, teaching and assessment. Her research interests lie in the evaluation of managed learning environments and associated educational developments, in particular with regard to institutional change.

Pamela Eastwood graduated from the University of Newcastle upon Tyne with a degree in agricultural and food marketing. She then worked in the agricultural and food industries in the UK and several other European countries before returning to her studies. She has recently gained her Ph.D., which was initiated at the University of Bradford's Food Policy

Research Unit and completed at Southampton Institute's Business School. Pamela is registered disabled and has personal experience of the application of ICT to ameliorate her difficulties. She currently works for Citizens' Advice.

Margaret Fain is Assistant Head of Public Services at Kimbel Library, Coastal Carolina University in South Carolina. She is co-ordinator of the Library Instruction Program there and has presented as a panelist on successful instruction programmes at the Library Orientation Exchange Conference (LOEX) in Ypsilanti, Michigan. She received her MS in LS from the University of Chapel Hill. Her professional interests centre on creating effective user education programmes in a constantly evolving technological environment.

Stephen Fallows is Research Coordinator at the Centre for Exercise and Nutrition Science at University College Chester. His primary responsibilities involve the management of the research phase of a highly successful international M.Sc. programme that is delivered in Chester, Hong Kong and Singapore. He makes extensive use of ICT in support of students located around the world. He was previously Reader in Educational Development at the University of Luton. His involvement with ICT in teaching began in the late 1980s when he was manager of the pioneering ELF project at the University of Bradford.

Eveline Fallshaw began work as a computer programmer in medical research and since then has worked in six universities in Europe, Africa, Asia and Australia. She has over thirty years' experience in teaching, research, policy formulation and planning, and has been involved in the development, evaluation and continuous improvement of university quality assurance systems in Australia and in Hong Kong. Her research has focused on identifying the impact on quality in universities of shifting sources of funding. She is currently Associate Dean (Academic Development) for the Faculty of Business at RMIT University in Melbourne. She was previously responsible for the alignment of her institution's IT strategy with its vision for teaching and learning. This included the development of quality assurance processes for the integration of ICT into the curriculum with a view to optimising the benefits to the learners as well as to the university.

Jane Field established her own consultancy business in 1994, specialising in project evaluation, community development and capacity building, education, training and development, and European project management. She was the external evaluator for four university-based ADAPT-Ufi projects, all of which addressed the use of ICT for learning. She was a consultant for Oracle UK, supporting the development of Think.com, web-enabled software and developing and moderating the 'Teacher Zone', an online community.

Jonathan Foster is Lecturer in Information Management in the Department of Information Studies at Sheffield University. Previously he was a Research Associate on the Computer Based Collaborative Group Work Project. His teaching and research interests include information management; professional development for information management; information systems and organisations; and project management.

Marc Griffiths is Head of the Computer Studies Department at the H. Lavity Stoutt Community College in the British Virgin Islands. He is currently pursuing a Ph.D. which examines the impact of web-based distance education within the socio-economic context of the British Virgin Islands. He teaches computer programming, networking, CAPE computing and web page design.

Graham Hart joined the University sector in 1990 to lecture on business management after thirty years in industry, latterly at director level – this allowed him to pursue his interest in management development. A widening interest in teaching and learning and the use of ICT in enhancing the student experience led to his joining Ultralab in May 2000. He now supports academics across all schools in the design and delivery of ICT-based tuition both in the classroom and via distance learning. His research interest is ensuring that what is offered is pedagogically sound and not a mere copy of traditional course materials. He is a member of the university committee developing standards for online learning and teaching.

Jill Jameson is Director of Lifelong Learning at the University of Greenwich. This role involves the advancement of the university's involvement with the local community and the encouragement of education throughout life – rather than the traditional focus on school leaver entrants to university. She recognises that ICT-based initiatives will have significant importance in the advancement of these developments.

Gillian Jordan has a work focus in open learning within the School of Health at the University of Greenwich. Her background is in physiotherapy and she has extensive experience of both undergraduate and postgraduate education. She is responsible for developing open and distance learning opportunities for health professionals and is leader of the M.Sc. CPD (Health) programme. Her academic interests are in the areas of continuing professional development and the use of computers as communication tools. She is a member of the Chartered Society of Physiotherapy's Council, where she sits on the Education Committee, the Scientific Panel and the CPD and Lifelong Learning Panel.

Peter Kandlbinder works in the Institute for Interactive Media and Learning at the University of Technology, Sydney. Previously he was a lecturer in the Institute for Teaching and Learning at the University of Sydney. He has worked in a number of fields including desktop publishing, video production and secondary teaching. For more than ten years he has been involved in open, distance and flexible learning in Australia and the South Pacific. Most recently he has focused on developing flexible learning programmes for academic staff. He is currently co-ordinator of the Postgraduate Supervisors' Development Programme.

Arti Kumar is Senior Careers Adviser at the University of Luton, where she co-ordinates a Career Development Module for undergraduates. She took a degree in contemporary studies and a Masters in education while raising three sons and working part-time. She has worked in a variety of occupations in the past, and in careers education, information and guidance. She is enthusiastic about all aspects of careers education – designing, delivering and assessing it – and leading developments to integrate it into the higher education curriculum.

Vic Lally is a researcher, teacher and lecturer with twenty years' experience in the fields of secondary and higher education. He is Director of the Science Education M.Ed. programme. He is Co-Director of the Computer Based Collaborative Group Work Project and a founder member of the Centre for the Study of Networked Learning at Sheffield University.

David McConnell is Professor of Networked Learning in the School of Education and Co-Director of the Computer Based Collaborative Group Work Project at Sheffield University. He has worked at Lancaster University (Centre for the Study of Management Learning), Bath University, the Open University (Institute for Educational Technology), Murdoch University, Perth, Western Australia and Surrey University.

Carmel McNaught is Professor of Learning Enhancement at the Chinese University of Hong Kong. Her previous appointment was Head of Professional Development in Learning Technology Services at Royal

Melbourne Institute of Technology in Australia. Carmel has had twenty-eight years' experience in teaching and research in higher education in seven universities in southern Africa, Australia and Asia. She integrates her staff development programme with working as an educational designer and evaluator in specific projects where staff are using communication and information technologies. She has published extensively in this area. Another field of research involves looking at relationships between academics' beliefs about teaching and learning and their design, and the use of computers in teaching and learning.

Christine Steven has experience teaching in secondary and further education as well as higher education. Her subject specialism is computer science but she maintains an interest in pedagogic issues and much of her research is in this area. She was for some years a Teaching Fellow at the University of Luton, where much of her work centred on issues of assessment, with particular emphasis on the use of computer-aided assessment packages and their effectiveness. She is now a teacher in a secondary school in Kent where she has responsibility for key skills development and the use of computer-aided teaching and assessment.

Vic Tandy is Experimental Officer in the School of International Studies and Law at Coventry University. His role is to provide advice and support to staff in the development of computer-enhanced teaching materials. He also contributes to the development of information systems across campus. His teaching responsibilities cover the integration of IT with subjects taught in the school. He is also an active researcher, and has discovered a link between low frequency sound and feelings in humans that may be interpreted as a paranormal event. Described in some areas as the 'Tandy Effect', the implications of this research could be profound.

Stan Zakrzewski works in the Department of Computing, Information Systems and Mathematics at London Metropolitan University. He was previously Head of Research (Learning Resources) at the University of Luton where he managed the implementation of computer-based assessment at the university and researched implementation models for computer-based course delivery and assessment.

Series editor's foreword

This is the partner volume to *Educational Development Through Information and Communications Technology*, also in the SEDA series and by the same editors. It significantly adds to the work that Stephen Fallows and Rakesh Bhanot have done to help so many of us navigate our way through this important area of higher education.

It is becoming clear that the growing range of information and communications technologies are not tools or processes that we are able simply to incorporate into our existing practice without significant change. For some of us this is good news, and all through higher education there are examples of colleagues using the occasions offered by ICT development to stimulate deep and thoughtful review of fundamental principles. For others, such changes are to be handled with care, as they may put at risk the standards, quality, pedagogy and reputation that have been carefully built up over many years.

One of the pleasures of reading the contributions in this present volume is their range and diversity. Quality issues in using ICT are matters of concern in all HE systems, and developing an international perspective on them is important. At the same time, ICT is affecting all aspects of the student experience, challenging the exclusivity of the teaching space and redefining the opportunities for learning. SEDA is committed to supporting its members and others in higher education to think through the challenges and to work to improve the quality of students' learning. I welcome the opportunity that Stephen Fallows, Rakesh Bhanot and their contributing authors have given us to engage in this work.

James Wisdom
SEDA Series Editor

Preface

This book is the second of a pair of linked volumes – the first – *Educational Development Through Information and Communications Technology* – was published by Kogan Page in 2002.

The first volume focused on a series of case examples that detailed how institutions, departments and individuals have incorporated ICT modes of curriculum delivery into their programmes. This second volume is concerned with mechanisms which will help to ensure that educational quality is not compromised as ICT approaches are adopted. That is, ICT-based work is of at least equivalent quality to that which it replaces.

Chapters address quality matters in a variety of ways; for example:

- Processes that need to be addressed as an institution decides on its institution-wide ICT in teaching strategy.
- Examination of an institution's strategy and procedures to embed quality assurance procedures into the development of ICT-based materials.
- The impact of initiatives from external quality assurance agencies with reference to ICT programmes.
- Quality in distance ICT programmes and in support of research.
- The ways in which the adoption of ICT has assisted the disabled student to participate more fully in higher education than was previously the case.
- Maintaining quality of assessment when ICT-based approaches are adopted.
- How to ensure that student work is genuine in an age of ICT-based routes to cheating.

Ensuring quality also requires other professional support processes, and the book provides a selection of case examples:

- Dealing with ICT anxiety.
- Networking of professional development.
- Use of ICT in staff development and training.
- ICT support for postgraduate supervision.
- Support for students and colleagues through e-Mentoring.

We know that we haven't included every issue with respect to ensuring quality of provision in higher education – rather this set of examples is illustrative of the broad range of aspects of higher education that ICT now impacts upon. It is our view that when used appropriately ICT can make a positive contribution to many (if not all) areas of higher education.

Stephen Fallows and Rakesh Bhanot

Acknowledgements

The editors of this book have sought advice and comment from a wide range of colleagues within higher education. We do not intend to name specific individuals (not least because we would hate the embarrassment that we would have to endure if we missed someone).

But a big thank you to everyone who has assisted us in getting this book from its genesis through to publication.

1

Quality in ICT-based higher education: some introductory questions

Stephen Fallows and Rakesh Bhanot

SUMMARY

'Quality' is a difficult concept to define and one that is impossible to define with any degree of universal agreement. Almost every writer on the subject has used a personal favourite – this is as true of the contributors to this book as anywhere.

We do not intend to add to the definitions here, but rather will discuss a few of the key themes which emerge as writers consider quality in higher education and apply these to the specialist area of ICT-based education.

ICT-BASED EDUCATION

It is useful to review quickly what we understand by the term *ICT-based education*. Information and communications technologies represent the coming together of computers (information technology (IT)) with telecommunications technologies. The concept ranges from the relatively straightforward and now everyday use of computers for the production of teaching materials that will be used in a standard classroom situation to the transnational linking of learners around the planet for a shared learning experience that would have been quite impossible a generation ago.

As academics we have come to view ICT as such a basic toolkit that it is almost impossible for us to envisage how our predecessors performed their various duties of teaching, assessment and research without it. But, of course, the previous generations were taught and did learn without technology – some would even argue that the teachers were able to get on with their responsibilities with greater efficiency than their modern counterparts. Education thrived without everyone having to develop the additional proficiencies that are deemed essential in the twenty-first century.

However, most of us are not Luddites; we are willing to adapt to changing times even if not always keen to embrace every element of the new developments, but sometimes it is worthwhile to stand back and ask a few key questions:

- Can the use of ICT-based approaches enhance the quality of learning and teaching?
- Does the use of ICT-based approaches enhance the quality of learning and teaching? (Or are we using expensive equipment to achieve no more than our predecessors did with cheap and dusty chalk and talk?)
- How does the use of ICT-based approaches enhance the quality of learning and teaching?
- Are we (as teachers and learners) fully enabled to maximise the quality of the benefits that can arise from the use of ICT?

The contributors to this volume address these questions and others.

BASICS OF 'QUALITY'

A long established principle relating to the matter of quality is 'fitness for purpose' – thus the peasant farmer's hand hoe is appropriate for the task being undertaken by that farmer in exactly the same manner that the £100,000 tractor and associated set of implements is appropriate for the needs of the prairie farmer. Each farmer has a set of tools to do the job and each appreciates the quality of these tools. Giving the £100,000 tractor to the peasant farmer would not necessarily be appropriate and thus would not enhance quality.

This farming analogy transfers neatly into education. It is not simply the adoption of a new approach that enhances quality. Over the years, lecturers have progressed from use of chalk on a board to photographic slides through handwritten and typed overhead transparencies to presentation software such as PowerPoint. Effective use of each technique requires appropriate skills. The lecturer of a previous generation would be overwhelmed by the prospect of PowerPoint while today's lecturer who prepares detailed multimedia presentations could well be challenged if the 'props' of twenty-first-century teaching were to be removed.

Today's students arrive in higher education with quite different expectations and demands than was the case even just a decade ago. Students are consumers of education and as customers they expect a quality experience. These expectations are fuelled by technology and often there is unfair criticism of those who are not seen to be adopting the current technologies. Teaching must be 'fit for the purpose' of meeting the expectations of the twenty-first-century student, and undoubtedly for the 'Play Station generation' this involves the use of appropriate ICT. But we must always remember that while ICT may be used to enhance the presentation of materials, it is not always enhancing either the learning or the teaching – for instance, it is just as easy to use PowerPoint to present a poorly structured and inadequate lecture (which we would deem poor quality) as it is to use this technology to deliver a high-quality lecture with excellent structure and content.

PREOCCUPATION WITH QUALITY

Higher education in the UK gained a particular preoccupation with quality matters through the late 1980s and 1990s as institutions across the whole range of higher education sought to cope with the considerable expansion in student numbers without an accompanying expansion in physical resources and teaching staff. There has been a genuine and continuing fear that these circumstances would have an adverse impact on the quality of the educational process and the students' learning experience. The expansion in provision occurred concurrently with a shift in the organisation of higher education with the establishment of the so-called new universities; these re-badged institutions gained, for the first time, the in-house responsibility for their awards in the same manner as the previous generations of charter universities. New senior positions were established with a quality remit.

The preoccupation with quality has been somewhat clouded by a continuing confusion about the difference between quality and standards. Students have a right to an education that is consistent in the standards achieved by the different institutions; it is a core responsibility of each examiner to evaluate the extent to which standards are maintained. In some educational settings it is relatively simple to understand the nature of standards – the extent of a person's proficiency in a language may be measured in an objective manner while competence in the performance of a skills-based task (be it playing a musical instrument or undertaking surgery) can be similarly equated against defined standards. Standards may be less easily understood in other disciplines where objective measures are not so easily implemented (such as philosophy or even education itself).

The concept of quality is often linked with words such as 'assurance', 'enhancement' or even 'development'. Quality assurance focuses on

checking and evaluating to determine compliance with stated requirements and desired outcomes. The, more modern, terms *quality
enhancement* or *quality development* are concerned with seeking to achieve
something that is understood to be measurably better than that which
went before. Used appropriately, ICT can enhance the quality of the
students' learning experience but, if not used with due care and attention,
it can equally yield negative outcomes.

EXAMPLES OF ICT IN HIGHER EDUCATION – IS QUALITY BEING ENHANCED?

1 The electronic library

Institutions nowadays purchase the larger proportion of their journal
stock in electronic format. Furthermore, substantial electronic databases
allow materials to be identified almost instantaneously by use of just a few
keystrokes.

But is the quality of student experience enhanced? Each student is
enabled to access substantially more material than was previously the
case when everything was paper-based and more limited. Does more
mean better? The e-journal has clear benefits over the paper copy –
several readers both on campus and remote can use a single edition
simultaneously.

But does the students' tendency to accumulate a collection of printouts
that can be highlighted in a multitude of fluorescent colours develop
the fundamental research skills to the same extent as old-fashioned
reading and note-taking?

Does the instant access to information lead to plagiarism through the
simplicity of cut and paste?

We can see that the students' world has now shifted from a focus on
the search for information to a focus on the evaluation of the quality
of the mass of information that is now available to them. Quality use of
the electronic library in all its manifestations is a new skill that we each
have to acquire.

2 Technology improves presentation

Nowadays we have an expectation that students' work will be presented
in word-processed form. Students spend an age slowly keying in text and
preparing ever more sophisticated documents. Would this time be better
spent in other ways? (The same comment could be made about use of the
teachers' time.)

But is there a focus on style rather than on substance? Is the neatly word-processed document really of higher academic quality than the roughly typed or even handwritten manuscript? Is the use of PowerPoint presentation really a better (higher quality) mode of teaching than the old talk and chalk?

3 Email increases ease of feedback

We all use email to communicate with colleagues and increasingly with our students. We perceive emails as immediate messages that demand instant response. It can be appropriate for students to offer drafts of work via email or to ask questions on a range of issues, but the demands placed on us can be overwhelming.

Is email taking over our lives? The vast number of messages we all receive each day are taking over the working day (and beyond) – we all spend hours keying in our responses to often very trivial messages. Is the quality of our working lives being enhanced through this activity? Does it raise the quality of our outputs?

When our students are located at a distance then a quick and cheap means of communication is a genuine benefit. (SF has cohorts of students based in Hong Kong and Singapore and can confirm that the educational experience of these distance learners could not be truly equivalent to that of his UK-based students without use of email.) But, for on-campus students, does use of ICT bring genuine quality improvements over traditional modes of communication – is the electronic notice-board any more effective than the physical one with paper and pins?

4 ICT opens up educational opportunities

ICT is undoubtedly enhancing the options and opportunities for some learners. Distance learning harnessing the power of ICT is increasing at an exponential rate – similarly the use of distance learning techniques is a standard feature of many campus-based programmes of study. But is the shift from universal face-to-face delivery to the adoption of virtual learning environments enhancing the opportunities for all?

While ICT resources are available on campus, no institution can afford to purchase sufficient sets of equipment to ensure that all students may have unlimited access at all times. Increasingly, students feel the need to purchase their own equipment; while this may not be a problem for many, the additional financial outlay may prove impossible for others. Has quality been enhanced if students who could afford only a notebook and pen are to be excluded from the opportunities of higher education because they feel unable to afford a personal laptop and printer?

5 Is ICT only as good as the training offered?

Adoption of ICT requires training and development opportunities for both staff and students. While most of us get along with the technology through exploratory learning and perseverance, so much greater efficiency and efficacy would be achieved if the quality of training and development genuinely matched the quality of the equipment that we find on our desks. It is certainly not at all unusual for staff to be provided with thousands of pounds-worth of ICT equipment without a penny being spent on training or even basic instruction in its use. It is not deemed appropriate to develop our basic keyboard skills, and the 'hunt and peck' approach is widespread.

Is this a quality approach to the adoption of ICT? Proper skills development would maximise the effectiveness with which each ICT task is undertaken.

CONCLUDING COMMENT

The five examples cited above each pose challenges to institutions of higher education worldwide. We hope that the chapters which follow will give clues to solutions. There is clearly no instant solution and each of us will need to address the issues most appropriate to our requirements.

For the quality issues to be addressed, organisations will need to set in place systems to evaluate their local requirements, taking due credence of needs of all their learners and teachers. Similarly, learners and teachers will need to take personal decisions about what is appropriate action.

However, we believe that ICT may be used to raise the quality of education – but we also believe that it is not sufficient to merely purchase the equipment; it is also necessary to invest in development of the people who will use it whether these be teaching staff or students.

2

Moving into uncertain terrain: implementing online higher education

Frances Deepwell and Liz Beaty

SUMMARY

This chapter draws on our experience of over five years of research and development of Coventry's web-based, virtual learning environment 'Learn Online'. The introduction of 'Learn Online' may be viewed as a strategic educational development project and we begin the chapter with a description of the progress of the development through four phases over a five-year period. We go on to analyse important elements of risk management through broad issues of pace and timing of changes and the interplay between formal and informal management processes. In project management terms, the project has been approached from an action research and development stance. We have permitted the research findings to guide the development, both at the strategic and at the operational level.

INTRODUCTION

Learning online is fast becoming an important part of higher education. Universities are variously progressing their ability to harness this new information and communications technology to support their provision. As we write, however, few have taken the step, as Coventry University has done, to implement online learning across all modules and for all students. This chapter draws on our experience of five years of research and development of a web-based, virtual learning environment 'Learn Online'. Through a discussion of strategic direction, planning, implementation and evaluation we reflect on what our work reveals about managing the risks involved in this uncertain terrain. We describe the challenges, solutions and remaining issues in relation to matters of quality *assurance* in higher education.

The introduction of 'Learn Online' may be viewed as a strategic educational development project and we begin the chapter with a description of the progress of the development through four phases over a five-year period. We go on to analyse important elements of risk management through broad issues of pace and timing of changes, and the interplay between formal and informal management processes. In project management terms, the project has been approached from an action research and development stance. We have permitted the research findings to guide the development, both at the strategic and the operational level.

CHRONOLOGICAL OUTLINE

It is helpful to start with an outline of the chronology of development that has taken us from being an institution with dispersed pockets of innovative teaching to being one at the forefront of online learning practice, with over 50 per cent active usage in some subject areas. (Usage is determined on a module-by-module or course-by-course basis from hits registered on the WebCT server, adjusted to take student numbers into account.) There have been four broad phases of development: strategy formulation; piloting; launching a campus solution; evaluating and upgrading (see Box 2.1).

BOX 2.1   STAGES IN THE IMPLEMENTATION PROCESS

Phase 1   Strategy and choice of VLE   March 1997 to July 1998

Phase 2   Piloting   September 1998 to August 1999

Phase 3   A campus solution   September 1999 to August 2001

Phase 4   Evaluation and upgrades   August 2001 and ongoing

After a period of strategic planning with support from senior management, the University moved into a development and piloting phase during 1997–98. During this stage the scope of the virtual learning environment (VLE) was determined and the decision was taken that WebCT would provide the necessary platform. The decision-making process is described later on in this chapter (see the section 'Focus on pedagogy'). The intention to have a campus solution increased in urgency, and various responsibilities and projects grew from this including the need for a robust network infrastructure, the need to design the user interface and to provide suitable staff development. The following year (1998–99) was dominated by a large-scale pilot, involving Coventry Business School, the postgraduate programme for new lecturers, and other innovators across the university. During this year, the shape of the VLE was tested and refined, including the development of a standard template. In September 1999, just one year after the first pilot online courses, the VLE was fully implemented across the institution. The year 2000–01 saw the start of a systematic approach to evaluation and consolidation of usage. A significant upgrade in the version of WebCT was carried out at the start of 2001–02.

FROM INSPIRATION TO IMPLEMENTATION

The top-down strategic push towards exploiting ICT in learning was driven by the need both to maximise the benefits of innovations in teaching and learning and to harness the opportunities afforded by ICT. These two broad areas of educational development were articulated in an early version of a Teaching and Learning Strategy which, in 1997, was ahead of its time in the UK (HEFCE asked for Teaching and Learning strategies in 1999). The strategy included two separate, but interwoven, implementation plans – one focused on releasing time for academic staff to undertake development projects on teaching and learning – called the teaching and learning Task Force. The second sought to realise an 'electronic campus'. Since these two initiatives were running concurrently, they fed off each other and their influence within the institution was synergetic, both sharing as they did the common goal of enhancing the student experience.

IMPLEMENTATION PLAN 1: THE TASK FORCE

The teaching and learning Task Force was a rolling programme of inward investment established by the Pro-Vice-Chancellor (Teaching and Learning) in 1997. Each year, full-time members of teaching staff could apply for half-time secondment to pursue their own projects under the management of the Centre for Higher Education Development. The Task Force at times numbered up to twenty-five members and it became far more than the sum of its parts. Each member of the group was charged not only to undertake their own innovation project, but also to act as a champion for change within their local academic community. Members met regularly once a month in small action learning sets (McGill and Beaty, 2001) and at least once a term for a day as a whole group. While the action learning sets helped to support the development of individual projects, the large group meetings focused attention on identifying blocks within the institution that were hindering good innovations in learning and teaching practice. The communication between individuals and subject groups helped to bridge the gap between policy and practice (see Box 2.2).

BOX 2.2   QUALITY ISSUE – MODELS FOR COMMUNICATION AND PROBLEM-SOLVING

i A Sandwich model of educational development

Policy development

Staff development programmes

Staff needs

ii A hubs and spokes model of Task Force communication

The diagram below represents the many different subject specialists who have come together through the Task Force and shared their experiences with the aim of finding ways to move forward. Each member of the Task Force is also part of a local community and thus forms a moving wheel of communication within and across subject groups in the University.

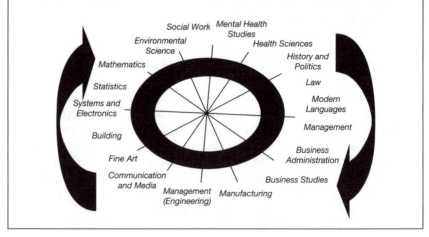

A crucial step was made to extend membership of the Task Force to include key people from support departments. They were referred to as Task Force supporters, and invited to all full meetings and included in the email list. This added to the effectiveness of the communication and prevented some of the 'us and them' attitudes that can get in the way of constructive conversations about change.

Not all of the Task Force projects were based around online learning but all included a pedagogical development. It was extremely useful to have academics who were not focused primarily on technological innovation intimately involved in its development. The neutral and sometimes sceptical attitudes within the group served as a moderating influence and a sounding board for planning: if members of the Task Force did not like an aspect of the development then the policy-makers knew they should think again. In effect the conversation also had the effect of influencing some of these sceptical colleagues in their own experimentation with the online environment and, as a result, some became the greatest champions for the technology. The learning point in this is the need for a robust model of communication. The Task Force has been so successful in bridging the potential communications barrier between policy and practice and between central services and academic subject areas that they have been praised in the recent quality assessment and quality audit reports:

> It became clear from discussions with staff and students that the innovations of the Task Force, particularly the introduction of WebCT (an on-line teaching and learning initiative), have already had a major impact on the working habits and the morale of the University, refreshing many courses and improving contact between lecturers and students.
>
> (Coventry University Quality Audit Report,
> June 2000)

IMPLEMENTATION PLAN 2: 'ELECTRONIC CAMPUS'

The concept of an 'electronic campus' emerged from investigations by senior members of the University. A small group had been to see other institutions in the USA and Canada and had been inspired by the slick administration delivered by Internet technology. On their return, they commissioned three members of the University to investigate all possible means to translate their vision into a reality for the University. A recommendation on how to implement a VLE was approved by the Vice-Chancellor's group, although the timescale for delivery was brought forward by twelve months from two years to one. Consequently, an implementation committee was established, chaired by one of the Deans of School, with three subgroups: User Interface, Systems Integration, and Training and Support. The three subgroups were chaired by the Pro-Vice-Chancellor so that the recommendations made could be acted upon at the highest management level. Membership of the groups was drawn from central support services and the Task Force. Simultaneously, Computing Services established an internal 'project board' to allocate resources to develop the technical infrastructure.

Alongside this formal mechanism, discussions about the implementation abounded. Members of the Task Force used both an email list and a discussion forum to raise issues and concerns relating to the introduction of WebCT including their feedback from pilot activity (see Cousin and Deepwell, 1998). Another relationship was also emerging during this phase, namely a constructive dialogue between the Centre for Higher Education Development and Computing Services. At the time, Computing Services had a reputation for serving the administration of the University. Requests for changes in standard software to facilitate teaching and learning were invariably passed over; outdated operating systems were delivered to student and staff desktops; and security restrictions imposed a complete divide between services to academic and administrative staff.

SOFT CONTROL AND THE PACING OF CHANGE

Change requires a champion. The importance of such a champion is not simply in the vision and leadership they command but also in their ability to protect those who are in the vanguard of change and to harness sufficient resources to enable change to happen. The Senior Pro-Vice-Chancellor has been this champion for Learn Online at Coventry University. His approach has been seen not only in the design of the Task Force strategy and in the promotion of the Centre for Higher Education Development, but also in his willingness to contribute to a two-way communication process across many layers in the institution. It has been as important to be a listener as it has to be a visionary. These changes have been embedded more effectively through the Senior Pro-Vice-Chancellor taking seriously the concerns of staff and being prepared to push changes without overly controlling them. A partnership with the Task Force has built trust and retained energy for the developments, which have not been without their pain. The early adopters in particular have had to live with failed experiments, wrong turnings and wasted efforts along the way.

Similarly, moving from early adopters to the critical mass envisaged for this serious investment has required a careful balance. On the one hand, the champions of innovation have exerted a tenacious and irrepressible pressure for change but, on the other hand, they have been able to concede and, on occasion, retract from over-extending the acceptable limits (see Box 2.3 for an example of retraction in the face of widespread opposition). In a climate where use of the VLE is gently encouraged and centrally supported, colleagues have been able to focus their efforts on using it to enhance the students' learning experience.

BOX 2.3   QUALITY ISSUE – MANAGING THE PACE OF CHANGE THROUGH ACTIVE LISTENING

When it was first proposed that each module would be represented in the VLE, there was a flurry of rumours that use of the online environment would be made compulsory. A poorly worded announcement in the University monthly briefing sheet exacerbated the situation. A public retraction was forthcoming: there would be no general compulsion for usage from top-level management.

A few individual subject groups took a more directive stance for their own area from the outset. Towards the second year of operation, however, loose targets were announced for the coming year. These targets were locally varied and based on observed trends in usage.

PACE OF CHANGE

As the implementation of the online facility proceeded, it emerged that different groups in the institution wanted a different pace of change. As a whole, the institution could be deemed 'ready' for the implementation; however, there was great variation at a more local level. There were those who wanted rapid developments so that they or their students could benefit from the new technology immediately; they wanted to be at the forefront of development, experimenting with new techniques and exploring the potential gain the technology brings, be it educational, competitive advantage or administrative. There were also those who wanted slower progress so that they could adapt their practice and procedures more gradually; this group has been less prepared to take risks and includes cautious administrators, overburdened teaching colleagues and computing support. A further group comprises those who resist change; initially these centred mainly around registration and financial areas of practice.

Managing diverse needs and keeping the majority on board with the change process requires skill and rapid adaptation. An example of this need occurred during our pilot year, 'Year Zero'. This was in fact a critical incident and impacted substantially on further developments. Members of the Task Force, among others, had been experimenting with the online learning environment. Their feedback was helping the Centre for Higher Education Development to restructure and finalise the institutional template and support materials. The initial template was a fairly sound design, but some things needed to be altered. Towards the end of the year, at a Task Force 'away day', the pilot group learned that they would not be able to carry their complete online modules over into the new academic year in their current form, due to the minor changes in the template. This realisation was very painful for them and invoked a lot of criticism of the implementation plan. Some were ready to abandon the project. The pilot users had accepted substantial change in the previous months to their methods of teaching and learning – however, they felt that this was one change too far. The change was ameliorated by members of the Centre for Higher Education Development who offered to assist them in transferring their materials manually and re-creating their module as it currently existed on the new system. Importantly for the change process, these conciliatory gestures by the Centre for Higher Education Development were acceptable and support for the central initiative was revived.

FOCUS ON PEDAGOGY

Both the Task Force and the online learning initiatives eventually had their home in the Centre for Higher Education Development. The Head of Learning Development, whose primary task has been to set up and manage the Task Force, became the Director of the new Centre in 1999 and was thus able to combine the Teaching and Learning Strategy within functions which contained online learning support, academic staff development and educational research. Placing the development of online learning firmly within an educational development brief ensured the primary focus on pedagogy. The critical mass of users was extended organically via the staff development programme for new academic staff (the professional development course made particular use of WebCT in its delivery and these colleagues therefore experienced online learning as students). An annual staff conference promoted the technology through showcase exhibitions, workshops and debates. A consensus around the university's strategy began to build organically through a community of practice encouraged and facilitated by CHED and an active core staff, including the distributed effort of the Task Force, promoting and problem-solving the implementation throughout the University.

Crucial to the implementation was the process by which the platform for the VLE was selected. At the time (1998) an awareness of web-based enhancements to teaching was only just emerging in higher education in the UK. The educational developers collected some comparative studies of available learning systems but found the majority to be approaching comparisons from a technical rather than an educational or philosophical stance. Hence the checklists were function-oriented rather than user-oriented (either for tutors or students). A detailed debate over a number of Task Force meetings culminated in a discussion of the features that academic colleagues regarded as essential in a teaching tool. From this discussion, we designed an evaluation checklist to structure the assessment of available web-based applications. Using this quality indicator, WebCT was found to fulfil far more of the criteria than any other integrated online environment at the time (see Box 2.4), and was thus considered by a substantial group of staff to be fit for the purpose.

BOX 2.4   QUALITY ISSUE – CRITERIA FOR JUDGING SUITABILITY OF A VLE

Among members of the Task Force there was a well-articulated dialogue on the technology and the pedagogy. The group was greatly concerned with the maintenance of academic quality in any process of implementing the technology: letting the pedagogy drive the technology, as one member put it. For this reason, we instigated a quality-control mechanism in our decision-making process. A list of essential features was compiled in consultation with the group against which all VLEs would be assessed. The list was the basis for online and face-to-face discussions and is summarised below:

ONLINE LEARNING ENVIRONMENTS: A CHECKLIST OF ESSENTIAL FEATURES

- Both parts of the user interface, student and staff, must be easy to use.
- Meaningful feedback to students must be possible.
- Staff must be able to update their online materials directly without having to ask an administrator to do it for them.
- Student progress, both in terms of their assessment results and their use of the content, must be available to staff.
- Students should be able to take self-assessments separately from the main assessment.

- Groups of students should be able to collaborate online.
- Online discussion groups should be supported.
- Online assessment should be enabled through the system.
- The system should 'flag' changes which have been made since the last time the student visited the site.
- Students should be able to record their own notes.
- Staff must be able to place links to external URLs from within their pages. Links to other pages within the module material must also be possible.
- It should be possible to have a Frequently Asked Questions section.
- Good online help should be available to both staff and students.
- The system must be accessible both on- and off-campus. It should not require users to have any unusual or expensive software or hardware.
- It should be viewable using industry standard browsers. Content should be able to be prepared using industry standard editors.
- Students should be able to print out course content for off-line study.
- A very high level of security is required; only students who are registered on the module should be able to view the online material.
- It should support multimedia features such as audio and video.

CHANGING PEDAGOGY – PEER CONTRIBUTION TO LEARNING

One of the more challenging issues to arise following the universal availability of online learning is a shift in student:tutor and student: student interaction. As one colleague says, it 'allows students to support their peers effectively' (Deepwell, 2001).

The online learning environment within our institution establishes a reliable structure for communication and information among the local academic community. Alongside the facilities to archive materials (course content) and to document processes (assignment details), there are also ways to build courses/modules through discussion and inputs from learners (discussion groups, shared areas). This opens up the avenue to meta-cognitive processes and reflection, both of each individual's own learning and of the contributions made by their peers and their tutors. This marks a move towards networked learning and can have a significant impact on conceptions of the role of tutor and student.

Examples are becoming widespread throughout the institution, and in some subject areas it has impacted on the delivery of the curriculum across entire courses. This is not to say that there is no resistance to the changing role of the tutor in this process. The VLE implemented at

Coventry can, by its very nature, be used flexibly. It provides a set of tools that tutors can decide to use or not use as they see fit. This means that it can be applied in a range of teaching styles, including the 'jug and mug' mode where the information is delivered to the students with the expectation that they will read it and absorb the material (see Box 2.5). However, the message from educational developers has been to embrace a student-centred and inclusive learning style.

BOX 2.5   QUALITY ISSUE – MANAGING STUDENT DIVERSITY THROUGH A VIRTUAL LEARNING ENVIRONMENT

An example of where the changing pedagogy has yielded a positive outcome for students is in a level 3 module in information design. The task was to create a file in a particular format, drawing from research into similar file layouts. Each student placed their file in their own personal project area for peer review. The learners commented constructively on each other's projects and were then able to modify their file in the light of peer feedback. Learners were, in effect, managing their own tutorials online through the virtual learning environment.

TEACHING QUALITY – PEER REVIEW

With the advent of the teaching quality assurance processes and requirements for peer observation and review has come an awareness that tutors can learn from each other. This can be facilitated through the VLE with tutors 'inviting' colleagues into their private module areas to show them what it is that they and their students have been doing online. This has perhaps been one of the greatest shifts to be seen among our colleagues. Before the introduction of the VLE, there were protests at the idea that other colleagues could intrude into a private teaching environment online. So the design of our VLE ensured that only those tutors responsible for teaching a given module were permitted access to that module. As time has gone by, however, there have been an increasing number of instances where colleagues have wanted to show off what they have achieved, or give others an insight into how they have approached a particular topic or method online. This has happened across subjects and across schools within the University. Such a sharing of teaching methods and practice has been highly productive for those involved, and has also resulted in joint presentations and publications on contrastive or similar approaches between disciplines (Davidson and Orsini-Jones, 2002).

ENHANCING THE IMPLEMENTATION

Evaluation has been a continual concern through the implementation process and has been used to enhance most areas of development. The evaluation strategy was defined early on in the development at three levels:

1   inform further developments in the implementation
2   inform university processes and procedures
3   inform wider HE community

The framework adopted by CHED for an institutional evaluation of the implementation of the virtual learning environment has been written up elsewhere (Deepwell and Cousin, 2002). In brief, the framework allows for a conversational and participatory but structured analysis of evaluation research (structured conversational approach to evaluation (SCATE)). The approach draws on the data matrix from Stake's countenance model of evaluation (Stake, 1967) but has incorporated processes and values from action evaluation (Rothman and Friedman, 1999). In the evaluation research, aspects of participant intentions are compared to what is observed at a number of key stages in the development. The findings are discussed with participants in a process of feedback and feed forward at early stages of the research. A further distinctive feature of this evaluation approach is that we have used the web to disseminate findings in three-dimensional format. While the institutional evaluation rests within CHED, the approach allows for involvement from across the University, either formally or informally.

Since 1999 when the full-scale environment was launched, there have been a number of significant developments as a result of some of the research findings. An example is the further extension of the student body to include students from partner colleges and work-based learners in the second year of operation.

Other enhancements to the implementation centre on the use of the personalised entry page to the students' modules and courses.

EASING THE ROUTE TO ADOPTION

The decision to develop just one solution university-wide rather than to support a number of solutions was a crucial one. The decision enabled us to channel resources into providing university-wide support for the single solution including, for example, the production of training materials, technical assistance, student induction sessions, software development and links with the institution's management information system.

Substantial effort went into assisting adoption through the design of the environment itself. This may be summarised under three broad headings:

1 customised template
2 automated module creation
3 automated student registration

By basing each module on a common template, the implementation ensured a baseline standard within each online module and maximised access to generic and centrally held learner support websites (see Box 2.6 for a fuller discussion of the use of the template). Through the design of the template we were able to promote a preferred method of using the VLE, namely one that focused on communication and resources rather than using it as an archive of lecture slides.

BOX 2.6 QUALITY ISSUE – A COMMON LOOK-AND-FEEL

Each module in WebCT was created based on one of the School templates. This enabled the design team to write generic help documentation and also provided a common starting point for all modules in WebCT. Each module carried its correct (i.e. registry-approved) title throughout, was shown in the appropriate School colour scheme and offered a reliable navigational structure for users. Tutors are still able to modify the template in its entirety (e.g. reorganising the page layout, changing the colour scheme, adding or removing any of the WebCT tools (discussions, calendar, assessment and so forth)). Importantly, however, the tutors are not faced with having to design the layout from scratch, or make decisions about which tools to include before embarking on the module. This is of particular benefit to those colleagues who are coming new to online learning and are just starting to formulate their own conception of such a medium. Another major benefit of the template approach is that it has enabled the institution to provide handy links to central university learning support areas, such as library and study skills websites from within the learning environment, as well as a direct link to detailed module information. Previously, such sites have been nested deep in the information jungle of the University corporate website.

SUPPORTING THE USERS: STAFF AND STUDENTS

With the introduction of a VLE, the institution was taking a new departure at a macro level and also expecting a change in learning and teaching at the micro level. Across the board this created a need for awareness and skills development, starting from a fairly low base in most areas. However, the VLE is a computing application that is designed for an educational context, and colleagues have, on the whole, readily understood the analogies with face-to-face teaching. From an educational development perspective, our stance is to value the pedagogic approaches employed by our colleagues and to recommend ways to adapt these to online interactions. Generally speaking, the maxim pertains that a good tutor is a good online tutor. Furthermore, over time it has become evident that the VLE users are increasingly sophisticated in their use and understanding of online learning.

As stated above, the template approach simplified the production of generic training materials for both staff and students. In order to address the diverse development needs of academic colleagues and support staff, we devised a range of methods and products, including a web-based support system, reference guides, information sheets, email, phone and drop-in sessions alongside presentations and hands-on workshops. Increasingly, the majority of educational development which takes place is in response to individual or small-group development needs. There are three colleagues in the Centre for Higher Education Development and another handful of colleagues spread over the Schools who support colleagues in the use of the VLE.

Student support is focused around the Computing Services Helpdesk and a universal induction session. We devised a handy leaflet – A4, three-fold – with essential logging-in information, and this was distributed to all new learners before arriving at the University. On arrival, in induction week, a hands-on session is timetabled for all learners. The session is generally built around a self-study guide supported by student helpers. In the current year we distributed well in excess of 5000 copies of the guide, mainly to first-year students in the September induction week.

UNRESOLVED ISSUES

We have come a long way very quickly in recent years. However, there are still some issues to be addressed which we will raise at this point with the qualification that we are already moving towards solutions. These outstanding issues are:

- *Staff workload*
  At the moment, staff workload is calculated on numbers of contact hours. This means face-to-face contact and only in one or two localised

instances has this been revised to include online contact with students. It remains a disincentive for colleagues to invest their time and energies in online learning.

- *Extension of Learn Online to support student profiles*
  The entry page to Learn Online provides an opportunity to personalise information based on a student or staff log in. This could be further developed into an individualised portal.

- *Moving with product upgrades*
  We have bought a commercial product, and as such are dependent on the company philosophy and pricing structures for annual licences. We are also subject to pressure to upgrade as newer versions of the VLE are released.

- *Student demand for consistency*
  Dealing with student demand for consistency within and across subject groups. This is one of the single, most dominant complaints from students who use the VLE and concerns the lack of consistency of usage from one module leader to another.

- *Distance learning*
  As a revenue source, distance learning is highly appealing. As an academic development, distance learning remains highly contentious.

- *Work-based learning*
  Increasingly, applied courses are delivered in a number of ways including work-based learning. The issues here are allied to distance learning.

CONCLUSION

The certainties that emerge from this analysis of our implementation of online higher education are far outweighed by the measure of uncertainty. The teaching and learning strategy which underlies the process is one that seeks to *manage* rather than to *control* change in our institution. Formal structures have been established; however, it is apparent that it is an informal network which enables them to operate successfully. At Coventry we have been fortunate to have a lively and capable informal network that has monitored and tempered the implementation process.

REFERENCES

Cousin, G. and Deepwell, F. (1998) *Virtual Focus Groups in the Evaluation of an Online Learning Environment.* ELT 98, University of North London. Available at http://www.unl.ac.uk/tltc/elt/elt98.pdf (accessed March 2003).

Davidson, A. and Orsini-Jones, M. (2002) 'Motivational Factors in Students' On-line Learning', in S. Fallows and R. Bhanot (eds) *Educational Development Through Information and Communications Technology.* London: Kogan Page.

Deepwell, F. (2001) *Introducing an Online Learning Environment across Coventry University.* Interim Report on Data 1999/2000. Available at http://www.coventry.ac.uk/ched/research/evaluation/index.htm (accessed March 2003).

Deepwell, F. and Cousin, G. (2002) 'A Developmental Framework for Evaluating Institutional Change'. *Educational Developments,* March, 2.5.

McGill, I. and Beaty, E. (2001) (rev. 2nd edn) *Action Learning: A Guide for Management, Professional and Educational Development.* London: Kogan Page.

Quality Assurance Agency for Higher Education (2000) *Coventry University Quality Audit Report,* Cheltenham: QAA. Available at http://www.qaa.ac.uk/revreps/instrev/coventry/foreword.htm (accessed March 2003).

Rothman, J. and Friedman, V. (1999) Action Evaluation: Helping to Define, Assess and Achieve Organizational Goals. Presented at the American Association Conference in Orlando, Florida, and published on the Action Evaluation website. Available at http://www.aepro.org/inprint/papers/aedayton.html (accessed March 2003).

Stake, R. (1967) The Countenance of Educational Evaluation. *Teachers College Record,* No. 68.

3

Quality assurance issues and processes relating to ICT-based learning

Eveline Fallshaw and Carmel McNaught

SUMMARY

Many Australian universities differ from those in other parts of the world in their administration – their students live and work over large geographical areas and various state-based structures are well entrenched in Australian experience. Quality assurance of distance education using traditional methods with little or no face-to-face contact is therefore not new. However, the appropriate adoption of the various types of ICT for flexible delivery poses a new challenge to build on what has been learned in the past and to develop relevant new processes which will satisfy students by delivering high-quality learning outcomes. It involves for the first time a reliance on robust technology which is simple for students to use and easy for academics to adopt and integrate in ways which enrich learning. The demands ICT places on staff development accompany the need to rethink ways to assess and assure the quality of the courseware produced using these technologies, and of assessing and evaluating student learning outcomes.

QUALITY AND ORGANISATIONAL STRUCTURE

An understanding of the importance of organisational culture in universities is important in designing quality assurance processes to apply to the use of ICT in teaching and learning, in making sure they are appropriate, and in being confident that they will gain acceptance. Effective management of universities is improved when the values of professional groups with strong shared cultures align with the organisational culture of the University. The design of quality assurance processes in teaching needs to take account of the values and roles of such groups, and to build on them from the top down and the bottom up, to maximise the effectiveness of such quality assurance processes. Universities traditionally work through coordination of collective decision-making processes, and this provides an important basis upon which issues relating to quality are played out (Millet, 1962 and Taylor, 1983, cited in Van Vught, 1989, p.14). Quality assurance systems should therefore reflect and build in processes that are empathetic to the following:

- Seniority and expertise as sources of authority that place high value on individualism.
- Self-management.
- Discretion over work.
- Self-regulation.
- Development of the profession.
- Strong belief in, and need for, autonomy.

Academics may comply grudgingly with quality assurance processes because 'it is the rule'; or they may comply because they have internalised the system as a reflection of their own values. It is only in the latter way that compliance will become self-sustaining without enforcement or policing (Handy, 1993). It is from such self-sustaining compliance that high-quality teaching and learning outcomes will come. The challenge is to design a system in such a way that it will become self-sustaining.

QUALITY BEGINS WITH IT PLANNING

The Royal Melbourne Institute of Technology University (RMIT) is one of Australia's major universities. It has a national and international reputation for its learning culture, the performance and employability of its graduates, the standards of its awards, its impact on a wide range of industries, and the outcomes of its applied research and development programmes. As budgets shrank and the demands of information technology grew, RMIT determined it was important that there was a coordinated and planned approach to maintaining and developing the significant investment already made in information technology and the supporting infrastructure to underpin its education and training activities.

RMIT and other universities confront similar issues concerning IT resource management and planning. IT in universities is a strategic asset which is increasingly critical to the delivery of teaching and learning. Increasingly, new students come to university prepared with a broad range of computing skills and with expectations of the provision of online services similar to those offered by other industries. The use of network and distance learning technologies allows RMIT to provide an anytime, anywhere, interactive and collaborative learning environment, but it brings with it the need to evolve appropriate organisational models to meet the learner's technology needs and assure quality.

An organisational plan for how to proceed is an important starting point. RMIT's Strategic IT Plan delivered a vision for organisational, technological and application strategies together with an implementation plan identifying a timetable and funding requirements. It provided a systematic approach to guiding RMIT's IT investments over time with the goal of achieving the desired teaching and learning outcomes. This Plan coordinated the requirements of the units within RMIT responsible for all aspects of ICT in education and training, and identified those functions which need to be coordinated through the development of policy to ensure effective and efficient integration of central and local IT systems and the optimum allocation and use of scarce resources. The importance of a stable technological platform in delivering student satisfaction with the use of ICT in learning cannot be overestimated.

In developing the IT Plan, an IT Alignment Project was undertaken to define the IT and process changes needed to allow RMIT to take advantage of the opportunities of the changing marketplace within education and training. The outcome of this project included a high-level process model, and identification of existing initiatives and of the gaps – in staff capabilities, in technology infrastructure, and in content and application systems – between the planned future and what was already being done. The second phase of the IT Alignment Project focused on implementing IT strategies, and developing objectives, time frames and resource requirements for education and training, and to bring coherence to existing initiatives. This included architecture and delivery platforms, user requirements for new students, and product delivery and management systems, and developing a coherent process for planning and implementation applicable to current initiatives and future projects. The planning methodology adopted in the development of the overall plan included certain stages. These provide a useful checklist for the development of IT plans to support the adoption of ICT:

- Identify the external factors that will affect and influence strategic directions.
- Identify IT trends and emerging technologies that the University could take advantage of over the next three to five years.
- Review and assess the current IT environment.
- Revisit the relevant aspects of the University's teaching and learning strategy that could be specifically enabled by IT.

- Identify and document a vision for IT.
- Identify the strategies and actions required to implement this vision, together with policies, projects, funding and resource requirements.

The factors fuelling the redefinition of education as distributed learning include re-skilling staff, growth of the non-traditional student markets, remote interactive technologies, and brokering arrangements with new partners. The challenge is to manage and meet expectations in the face of rising demand, while providing optimal IT support in a complex networked environment. The critical success factors underpinning high-quality learning using ICT lie in appropriate levels of standard-isation, integration and reliability offering a seamless foundation for individualised local environments for innovations in teaching and learning.

ALIGNMENT WITH TEACHING AND LEARNING

The strategies for managing IT need to be closely linked to the organ-isational structure, teaching, learning and business strategies of the University. For example, to maximise the overall effectiveness of IT in a manner aligned to RMIT's internal structure, it was determined that IT should continue to be managed differently depending on user needs in each Faculty rather than being centralised. However, it also required strong mechanisms to provide an overall IT framework across the University as a whole (Blanton *et al.*, 1992; Yetton *et al.*, 1997). The inte-gration of Faculty IT plans with that of the library was essential for access to digital information resources which nowadays underpin the curriculum. An effective integration mechanism was needed to promote feedback on IT performance and gain cross-functional participation in IT planning while facilitating communication among and between IT groups and user groups. This was particularly relevant to managing and developing ICT that requires considerable coordination across multiple stakeholders.

While there is a demand for low-cost, innovative, effective and efficient IT systems, this is likely to generate a natural tension as lower costs are normally associated with standardisation and centralisation, and innovation tends to be associated with decentralisation and devolved control. The solution for RMIT was to seek a balance between centralisa-tion and mandated adoption of standards, and devolution. It determined which activities and functions should be centralised and standardised and which should be devolved. The optimal model obtained the benefits of a centralised infrastructure without many of the disadvantages associated with a strong corporate control of IT. In particular RMIT is now obtaining the cost benefits of a common IT infrastructure without losing the benefits of user-driven IT innovation in teaching and research in the Faculties.

There are two features underlying this model – the shift from high-cost, fragmented systems proliferation to a common infrastructure, and the empowerment of users to run specialised local applications for teaching and research, and the ease of embedding and maintaining ICT across the curriculum. Once in place, a standardised infrastructure helps to maintain the users' current systems and their business unit independence, as well as giving them options for new courseware, and enabling integration and interoperability across the University where required. There is a significant advantage in introducing such an enabling infrastructure as it meets the needs for certain common teaching and administrative systems across the University, while supporting autonomous innovation in the faculties in IT for both on-campus and distributed teaching and learning.

Planning for the use of ICT is a crucial first step in assuring the quality of the learning outcomes for students. In particular RMIT's original plan made a number of specific stipulations to assure the successful implementation of the RMIT Distributed Learning System. The aims were as follows:

- To ensure that the student-centred teaching and learning focus was not compromised or subsumed by the technology.
- To build teacher and learner competencies and confidence that in turn ensured the appropriate use of technologies as part of the teaching and learning effort.
- To provide management processes to ensure quality outcomes and the effective deployment of resources to support associated design, development and evaluation activities.
- To deploy appropriate infrastructure, systems and support services.

It was therefore crucial to ensuring a student-centred approach to teaching and learning that quality assurance guidelines and measurable standards and performance indicators were established top down to adhere to standards, and bottom up to integrate with teachers' judgements on the appropriateness of the educational applications of the technology.

QA – TOP DOWN AND BOTTOM UP

While the academic hierarchy is usually 'democratic' and 'bottom up', and that for administration is normally 'bureaucratic' and 'top down' (Mintzberg, 1979), nevertheless university QA systems require a framework within which a large number of people, of more or less the same level of ability, work together in a common endeavour and share the same resources (Jaques, 1976). In reality, there are a number of stakeholders in the work of universities and some of these have different priorities and values. They include students, employers, teachers, managers, accrediting bodies, and society as a whole (Vroeijenstijn, 1991; Yorke, 1991; Harvey *et al.*, 1992; Berg, 1993; Frederiks *et al.*, 1994). Changes to ways of monitoring, assuring and assessing the quality of education are universal with increasing interest in value for money, accountability and greater access being commonly observed. ICT has the potential to allow greater flexibility in access, in choice of pace and place and in student choice of preferred learning style. Whether the teaching is predominantly electronically delivered, or a mix of both electronic and face to face, the concerns of stakeholders are similar: increased accountability and quality assurance with effectiveness in achieving the desired outcomes, preferably for the right price.

In general, when education provides valued outcomes to those involved, quality is judged to be high. A corollary of this is that quality has no real meaning except in relation to purpose or function (e.g. Ball, 1985; Reynolds, 1986). To find a secure basis to define quality in the use of ICT in teaching and learning, it is helpful to describe programmes of study as goal-directed. These goals then provide a framework by which quality may be assessed (De Weert, 1990).

While teaching quality will be judged good by whether or not it contributes to the achievement of purpose, the key question is: Who defines the purpose? If one's objective for a programme is about producing a highly trained workforce, then quality is measured by the ability of graduates to find work. On the other hand, if the programme design is judged on the basis of the efficient management of teaching provision, then non-completion rates and unit costs are appropriate measures. The view of the group wielding overall control over the quality assurance process will determine what is considered to be the best set of measures to indicate whether their purposes have been met.

QUALITY ONLINE: WHAT IS IT?

'How can a teaching/learning process that deviates so markedly from what has been practised for hundreds of years embody quality education?' This quotation is from the preamble to the Institute for Higher Education Policy (2000) report on benchmarks for success in Internet-based distance education; it encapsulates the huge changes that are rapidly taking place worldwide in teaching and learning practice. This case study of six US higher education institutions notes benchmarks that are seen as essential and benchmarks that are seen as *not* essential for ensuring quality online distance education. While the report focuses on distance education providers, we believe the findings are useful for institutions such as RMIT where most courses are taught by a mixed-mode approach of both face-to-face and online modes. The benchmarks that are considered essential relate strongly to the following:

- Clear planning.
- Robust and reliable infrastructure.
- Good support systems for staff and students, including training and written information.
- Good channels of communication between staff and students.
- Regular feedback to students on their learning.
- Clear standards for courseware development.
- Ongoing evaluation processes with strong student input.

None of these are surprising. It is the benchmarks that are considered *not* essential for ensuring quality online distance education that are more surprising to us 'old-school' teaching and learning advisers, such as:

- Catering for students' diversity of learning styles.
- Providing institutional rewards for effective teaching.
- Having a strong team focus on course design.
- Having collaborative and/or problem-solving activities.
- Taking a modular approach to course design where student mastery of each module is expected.

To summarise, the essential benchmarks have a strong focus on systems and process. The non-essential benchmarks listed here relate to diversity and richness of educational design. While one can read too much into one study, there are messages here about not allowing our universities to become online qualification 'factories' in order to achieve certain specified university targets. The challenge is to meet those targets while still developing and maintaining rich and stimulating learning environments for students.

We do not believe that we have *either* a purely pedagogical approach *or* a purely financial perspective; we need both. For example, RMIT is really seeing the move to online teaching and learning as a financial investment, on which the University expects to get a return, mainly in terms of quality assured courseware to support strategic offshore teaching. Each Faculty here has a list of its strategic programmes and major efforts are going in this direction. A Return on Investment (RoI) will occur only if the courseware we use is of high educational quality.

THE RMIT DISTRIBUTED LEARNING SYSTEM

RMIT has developed a Distributed Learning System (DLS) for online learning. Some of the principles underlying the development of the DLS are as follows:

- A suite of tools, not just one.
- Integrating educational principles into the description of the toolkit.
- IMS compliance of all tools.
- A team approach to online projects.
- Involvement of all seven Faculties in evaluating the toolkit and the effectiveness of the learning environments that are being developed.

We chose to go down the path of multiple tools to provide better functionality, so we are not using one product but a set of tools. These are largely commercial tools but we are also using a few tools developed in-house over the past two years. We have settled on the following set but we are aware that these tools will change constantly.

- The **Campus** (an in-house tool in use as a common gateway to the DLS for all registered staff and students).
- The **Classroom** (*BlackBoard CourseInfo*). This is a secure area, accessible through Campus, where registered staff and students can access learning materials and facilities connected with a particular subject in which they are enrolled.
- The **Community**. This is an area of the website designed to allow RMIT staff and students to be able to set up communication and discussion areas. (*BlackBoard CourseInfo* may be used, but *WebBoard* is also being provided. *Groupwise* is the RMIT choice for normal email.)
- **Critique** quiz tools (*Question Mark Perception*; and *WebLearn*, an in-house tool).

In order to develop staff capacity in using the DLS, a large-scale professional development exercise has taken place. This has involved time release (twenty-six days each), training and ongoing support for 145 staff across the University, two or three in each department. In this time release period academic staff develop online materials and support their colleagues in their departments to engage with online teaching and learning (McNaught and Kennedy, 2000).

SOME EVALUATION LESSONS

For evaluation we use the usual strategies of feedback from staff and students with email/online questionnaires, focus groups with staff and students, analysis of web access data, analysis of support/helpdesk records, and some analysis of performance on learning outcomes (McNaught *et al.*, 1999). At this stage we have little firm student performance data – indeed, we have only anecdotal evidence of learning enhancement (or otherwise).

Table 3.1 contains a list of positive and negative factors from two evaluation studies, which have a direct bearing on the online learning experience for students. Overall, despite the many problems they experienced, students remain positive about the future use of online learning, provided the difficulties are addressed.

One recent survey of 2462 final-year students across all faculties is interesting and illustrates this tension clearly. These are the students who have experienced all the 'teeting problems' of the system. Students were asked to indicate how much experience they had of online learning and then were asked to select adjectives to describe their experience – interesting, challenging, easy, enjoyable, accessible off-campus, flexible, suited my schedule, useful, relevant, helped my learning, difficult, lonely,

Table 3.1 *Positive and negative factors of the student online experience*

Positive factors	Negative factors
Convenience of communication with teaching staff	Technical problems
	Registration problems
Convenience of access to learning materials	Lack of contact with teachers
	Lack of contact with other students
Allows for self-paced learning	Poorly designed learning materials
Convenience of communication with other students	
Reduced travel to the institution	
Increased IT skills	
Induction programme	

Table 3.2 *Final-year students' perceptions of the usefulness of their online experience*

Useful?	None/of little use	Some use	A lot of use	Total
No	599	431	268	1298
	69.2%	48.2%	37.2%	52.3%
Yes	267	464	453	1184
	30.8%	51.8%	62.8%	47.7%
Total	866	895	721	2482
	34.9%	36.1%	20.9%	100.0%

frustrating, inconvenient, and unmanageable. The most common descriptions selected were 'frustrating' (41 per cent) and 'useful' (32 per cent). We then combined results for 'useful', relevant' and 'helped my learning'; as shown in Table 3.2, the greater the students' use of online learning, the more likely they were to indicate that it was useful.

Further, students who indicated that the experience of using online materials was frustrating used the materials less, and this pattern held across faculties. It does not appear that students' frustration was associated with the content of the materials. As many of the issues related to the technical and registration problems noted in Table 3.1 have now been solved, these data will serve as a baseline for a survey across all years of students.

LOOKING FOR ONLINE QUALITY

In late 2000 we conducted an audit of 530 online subjects in our DLS. There were seven review teams – one for each Faculty consisting of Faculty staff and staff from Learning Technology Services. Initially, there was a great deal of suspicion about this 'police' activity, but, by organising collaborative effort with staff in the Faculties, the exercise was seen as much as an evaluative feedback as being quality control. However, the tensions between the two can be a fine line! We did not look at all online learning environments at RMIT; the review teams did not look at subjects still undergoing development, at subjects 'switched off' because they were not currently operating, or at online materials which still reside on faculty and departmental servers.

We used a quality assurance checklist (outlined in Table 3.3) to do the audit. Only about half of the subjects were felt to be adequate, and feedback was given to all subject owners about where improvement could occur. This exercise was used to trial the checklists that are now incorporated into an online approval process. This basically asks staff to show

Table 3.3 *Topics in the quality assurance checklist for online subjects*

Section A: Educational planning and design of online environments

Topic	Some points to consider
Opportunities for interaction and communication	A feedback mechanism. At least one moderated discussion forum.
Flexible assessment and performance feedback	A current collection of assessment materials and supporting documentation. Samples of previous assignments/project work (with documented student permission) should be made available as well. A collection of past/recent exams and sample tests (where appropriate). At least one self-help quiz (for formative assessment purposes) per learning objective, topic or theme. Provision for electronic submission of assignment work.
Flexible academic administration and learner support	Direct access to the related approved subject guide. A current timetable/timeline related to outlining face-to-face tutorials, lectures, lab/fieldwork and online activities (with times, dates and location details). Online learning activities are clearly described/linked to curriculum outcomes. Current contact details of lecturers, teachers and tutors. A structured collection of frequently asked questions and/or glossary.
Flexible provision of quality learning resources	A structured collection of learning resources. Clear links to related library resources and databases. A structured and validated collection of annotated WWW links.

Section B: Online learning resource publishing standards

To be completed if the DLS subject contains a structured collection of online learning resources. Are the guidelines for the following areas addressed?

- RMIT intellectual property and copyright
- RMIT 'identifiability'
- Website and interface design
- Accessibility

evidence of some educational planning before their subjects become 'live' on the DLS. The Directors of Teaching Quality in each Faculty check that members of staff have indeed considered the design features of an online system, have thought about the overall rationale for the subject in question, and comply with basic publishing standards (including copyright matters). For staff involved in major strategic course renewal projects the quality approval process also involves peer review and the formulation of an evaluation plan.

KEY CHALLENGES

Our current key challenges for enhancing the quality of ICT-based learning relate to:

- Overcoming negative perceptions from early unsatisfactory experiences.
- Educational design and publishing standards.
- Timescale and workload.
- Getting take-up of the quality assurance processes.
- Maintaining momentum.

Overcoming negative perceptions from early unsatisfactory experiences

The following problems have been noted in all our DLS evaluations: access and authentication difficulties; perceived lack of confidence in DLS stability; lack of time and support; and unwillingness to put course material in the DLS until RMIT intellectual property policy is reviewed and promulgated. We have made significant progress with technical problems and have a much more satisfactory intellectual property policy. We now need to convince staff and students whose initial experiences with the DLS have not been optimal that a process of continuous improvement is in place. Continuing efforts with these issues will be needed for some time.

Educational design and publishing standards

There will be a need for support in this area for some time. Some examples of the issues that were noted in the DLS audit process and which need to be addressed are:

- Lack of clarity in linking resources and activities to learning outcomes.
- Lack of flexibility in catering for diverse groups of students.
- Lack of linking to strategic priorities (e.g. internationalisation, work-integrated learning).
- No links to activities; just the provision of resources.
- Extraneous buttons.
- Unclear navigation strategies.

In addition, a need to enhance the basic style used by many staff in their online spaces was noted. Many of them are boring, and that is not good educational practice. Further, the value that good multimedia design can bring to educational experience (Kennedy and McNaught, 1997) is not often realised. We continue to grapple with how to provide support for the use of appropriate 'learning objects'. Some of these may be third party, and our library is keen to work on sourcing these. Some may be custom-built simulations, small videos and so on. Staff need support for the development of these learning objects. We are building a collection of good practice examples from within RMIT that is available for staff within RMIT.

Timescale and workload

Setting unrealistic timescales for innovative work and too steep a learning curve about online learning are often cited by staff and do account for several of the fairly 'empty' DLS subjects we found during the audit process. The issue of staff workload is a major one in Australian universities (and elsewhere). It is a challenge that must be resolved.

Getting take-up of the quality assurance processes

We are pleased with the processes we have designed. There is little intellectual resistance to the need for evidence of planning process (including copyright and intellectual property sign-off). The response of staff at workshops has been positive. But it is another process to add to the workload of staff . . . and therefore another challenge to embed.

Maintaining momentum

We have a great deal of consolidation and development to do. We have a sense of gathering momentum. Several Faculties are showing real commitment, though a few may still need a persuasive nudge. Have we reached critical mass yet, where the high-quality use of technology will roll out across the University? Probably not, but we feel we are on the right track. We will see. . . .

REFERENCES

Ball, C. (1985) 'Fitness for purpose', in D. Urwin (ed.) *Essays in Higher Education.* Guildford: Society for Research in Higher Education and NFER-Nelson.

Berg, C. (1993) University autonomy and quality assurance. *Higher Education in Europe,* 18 (3), 18–26.

Blanton, J.E., Watson, H.J. and Moody, J. (1992) Towards a better understanding of IT organisation: a comparative case study. *MIS Quarterly,* 16 (4), 531–55.

De Weert, E. (1990) A macro-analysis of quality assessment in higher education. *Higher Education*, 19 (1), 57–72.

Frederiks, M.M.H., Westerheijden, D.F. and Weusthof, P.J.M. (1994) Stakeholders in quality: improvement or accountability in systems of quality assessment in higher education. Paper presented at the 16th European Association for Institutional Research Forum, Amsterdam.

Handy, C. (1993) *Understanding Organisations.* London: Penguin Books.

Harvey, L., Burrows, A. and Green, D. (1992) *Criteria of Quality.* Quality in Higher Education Project, University of Central England, Birmingham.

Institute for Higher Education Policy (2000) *Quality on the Line: Benchmarks for Success in Internet-based Distance Education.* Washington, DC: IHEP. Available at http://www.ihep.com/Pubs/PDF/Quality.pdf (accessed February 2004).

Jaques, E. (1976) *A General Theory of Bureaucracy.* London: Heinemann.

Kennedy, D.K. and McNaught, C. (1997) Design elements for interactive multimedia. *Australian Journal of Educational Technology*, 13 (1), 1–22. Available at http://www.ascilite.org.au/ajet/ajet13/kennedy.html (accessed February 2004).

McNaught, C. and Kennedy, P. (2000) Learning technology mentors: bottom-up action through top-down investment. *The Technology Source*, November/December. Available at http://horizon.unc.edu/TS/development/2000-11.asp (accessed February 2004).

McNaught, C., Kenny, J., Kennedy, P. and Lord, R. (1999) Developing and evaluating a university-wide online Distributed Learning System: the experience at RMIT University. *Educational Technology and Society*, 2 (4). Available at http://ifets.ieee.org/periodical/vol_4-99/mcnaught.html (accessed February 2004).

Mintzberg, H. (1979) *The Structuring of Organizations.* London: Prentice Hall.

Reynolds, P.A. (1986) *Report of the Committee of Vice-Chancellors and Principals – Academic Standards in Universities.* London: CVCP.

Van Vught, F.A. (1989) *Public Administration and Higher Education*, Publication No. 87. Higher Education Policy Studies. Enschede: Centre for Higher Education Policy Studies.

Vroeijenstijn, A.I. (1991) External quality assessment: servant of two masters? Unpublished paper presented at Conference on Quality Assurance in Higher Education, Hong Kong.

Yetton, P. and Associates (1997) *Managing the Introduction of Technology in the Delivery and Administration of Higher Education.* Evaluations and Investigations Program Report 97/3, Australian Government Publishing Service, Canberra. Available at http://www.detya.gov.au/archive/highered/eippubs/eip9703/front.htm (accessed February 2004).

Yorke, M. (1991) *Performance Indicators: Observations on their Use in the Assurance of Quality.* Project Report No. 30, Council for National Academic Awards.

4

External quality assurance initiatives: impact on ICT-based programmes

Graham Hart

SUMMARY

This chapter uses the example of guidelines suggested by the UK Quality Assurance Agency for Higher Education (QAA) some years ago to consider the impact that external agencies with a quality assurance remit can have on the development and implementation of ICT-based programmes. The suggested guidelines refer to distance learning but have clear application to any use of ICT in higher education. The chapter identifies several issues that those developing ICT-based programmes need to address.

INTRODUCTION

In the late 1980s and during the 1990s the public was voicing increasing concern about its perception of the failure of the education system to deliver perceived value for money. At the same time structural changes and increased funding for higher education took place in a general climate of central government demanding measurable improvement in educational performance. The era of league and performance tables was thrust on all sectors of education from primary schools through to universities. Various agencies appeared to measure, monitor, control and offer advice. While these changes may be derided by some as interference in areas of academic freedom, it cannot be denied that many of the *laissez-faire* and conservative attitudes prevalent in education could not continue unchanged. One of the products of this change in ethos is a guideline document on distance learning, issued some years ago in an attempt to ensure that the student experience changes for the better.

Comprehensive guidelines for the quality assurance of distance learning were issued by the Quality Assurance Agency for Higher Education (QAA) (1999). Although issued some years ago as generic guidance for all UK-sourced distance learning programmes, this document still provides a useful tool for the evaluation of ICT-based teaching and learning.

'Distance learning' has been taken to mean a way of providing higher education that involves the transfer to the student's location of the materials that form the main basis of study, rather than the student moving to the location of the resource provider. All ICT-based materials have the potential to be used in such a way, even though they may not have been originally authored for such use. Thus, such materials would fall within the scope of the guidelines that apply to materials designed for distance learning. The challenge will be for institutions to recognise this, identify the materials and apply the appropriate quality assurance processes. The QAA provided six guidelines that are set out well and clearly, and are very specific and quite demanding. The guidelines are supported by twenty-three precepts that are in turn associated with 116 guideline statements. Thus, the QAA may be seen as posting clear markers against which the institutions' strategies could be benchmarked. While some precepts may not apply to every module or course, the spirit and ethos of ensuring excellent student experience certainly does.

GENERAL IMPLICATIONS OF THE QAA GUIDELINES

The six guidelines cover the following:

1   System design – the development of an integrated approach.
2   The establishment of academic standards and quality in programme design, approval and review procedures.
3   The assurance of quality and standards in the management of programme delivery.
4   Student development and support.
5   Student communication and representation.
6   Student assessment.

These guidelines, taken together with the requirement to elicit a teaching and learning strategy, are seen by many academics as being bureaucratic in concept and diminishing traditional academic freedom. Closer examination shows, perhaps, that they establish a useful template to be used to design both the teaching and learning activities and the processes involved in the delivery and administration of courses. What is already emerging is the reality that these guidelines cannot be ignored. The word 'explicit' is used no less than seven times in the guidelines and their accompanying precepts. The repeated use of this word cannot be accidental; it is clearly designed to ensure that institutions critically examine existing attitudes and processes, and make the changes necessary to accommodate the accelerating move to distance learning. Adherence to the guidelines and the emphasis of the precepts should prevent institutional drift from traditional methods of delivery into computer-facilitated distance learning, without there being adequate processes in place. Attention is drawn to some of the guidelines and their precepts, which may well impose new duties on institutions. Certainly some of these precepts will challenge cherished and traditional academic and administrative attitudes. Examination of some of the guidelines and precepts, in detail, may help to expose some of the prevalent attitudes and processes and areas that will need change.

The choice of the words 'development of an integrated approach', in guideline one, covering 'System design – the development of an integrated approach', is interesting and cannot be accidental. It recognises the reality of what many institutions would rather not admit, namely that they have systems and processes which in isolation may be excellent but which together often have significant broken links. Most institutions would argue that they have clear vision statements and policies for realising those visions, yet their publication alone does not ensure either downward communication of those policies to staff or their adoption by staff. This is particularly the case where management strategies and processes appear to derive little from the high-level statements.

Experience in the UK, corroborated internationally by other practitioners, suggests that a frequently encountered model is one of pioneers developing their own online activities, in isolation and unsupported by policy or allocation of either resources or finance. Such activity is frequently concentrated on the technology that is perceived as new and exciting and a better way of doing things. This activity may be unguided by any appropriate pedagogical approach and at the same time totally divorced from the existing institutional processes of quality assessment. This happens not through a wish to circumvent the processes, rather because the pioneer slowly develops the material and then makes it available to students in parallel with his or her traditional teaching materials. Thus, drift occurs.

Institutions must establish policies in this area together with appropriate processes of management and quality assurance. Directorates need to recognise that such activity is a healthy and logical consequence of developing educational theory. There should be a warm welcome for such activity and an understanding of the need to facilitate change in the processes to embrace and foster the new paradigm. This is best done by developing the current processes to keep the best features and at the same time incorporate flexibility that will allow exploitation of the new methods of delivery and assessment to encourage pioneers in this area. Where institutional response to awareness of such activity is conditioned by a corporate culture based on rigidly applying current control processes, irrespective of their appropriateness, it is unlikely that the work of the pioneers will cease. They will continue, and migrate to more congenial surroundings.

A REVIEW OF SELECTED GUIDELINES AND PRECEPTS

Guideline 1, Precept 3

Prior to offering programmes of study by distance learning, an institution should explicitly design and test its system for administering and teaching students at a distance and plan for contingencies in order to meet its stated aims in terms of academic quality and standards.

In some institutions this precept will require a fundamental rethinking of the current inwardly focused administration processes that are hierarchically driven. Alien words such as *service* and *customers* will have to become part of the institutional vocabulary. Management will have to engineer profound changes throughout their institutions so that processes can become more interactive and service-centred. While module content will continue to be the preserve of academics, increasingly there will have to be rigour of processes of both delivery and administration, solely so that the quality of student experience is enhanced at best and maintained at worst. This will inevitably lead to tensions, as academics feel threatened by the loss of some perceived academic freedoms. Perceived, because they were never real: rather the freedoms that many enjoy are the product of poor management over time. Increasingly, to meet the QAA guidelines, management will have to develop and change processes so as to achieve consistency across programmes and schools and/or departments. Consistency becomes the watchword; quality of student experiences the yardstick of measurement.

While the overall precept refers specifically to distance learning, it is not logical to believe that this excludes ICT materials used as part of a traditionally delivered course. Processes 'in order to meet its [the institution's] stated aims in terms of academic quality and standards' are surely not the exclusive prerogative of the distance programmes.

Guideline 2, Precept 7

In designing distance learning programmes of study, and any component modules, a providing institution should ensure explicit and reasoned coherence between, on the one hand, the aims and intended learning outcomes, and, on the other, the strategies for teaching at a distance, the scope of the learning materials and the modes and criteria of assessment.

This precept recognises the shift from an instructional teaching paradigm (Barr, 1994) to a learning paradigm and the parallel move to a significantly student-centred culture. Such a change will be painful and threatening to many academics; others will welcome it. Adoption of this paradigm shift will require careful change in management, a skill not notably present in conservative organisations, and a process that is rarely well handled even by progressive organisations. Incorporation of ICT-based materials into traditional programmes may be the first steps in the move to a learning paradigm.

Module design for student-centred learning is an alien process to those used to teaching to module objectives. Distance learning is a different paradigm to standard face-to-face delivery and requires different approaches to student engagement. Designing integrated formative and summative assessments is significantly different to setting a traditional module end assessment. The formative assessment process, within a traditionally delivered programme, may be aided significantly by computer-based programmes. This assessment process may be used within the class environment or at a distance. Either way it must be integrated into the course design. Overall management will need to take positive and affirmative action to ensure that appropriate staff development takes place in support of the move to a learning paradigm and the likely parallel move to ICT materials.

Guideline 2, Precept 9

A providing institution should have processes for approving distance learning programmes of study which, while underpinned by principles relevant to all educational programmes, take specific account of the requirements of the system of distance learning adopted and of the opportunities provided for scrutiny.

This precept recognises the obvious: that distance learning is different to classroom-based learning. It also requires that institutions acknowledge this and act accordingly by moderating existing, or adopting new, processes. This may be comparatively simple, if time consuming, with traditional paper-based programmes. Such programmes have been in use for decades and various models well proven. The evaluation is perhaps less easy with web-enabled distance learning, not least perhaps because the practitioners are not many in number and the processes of best practice are, like the technologies themselves, emergent. It is important therefore that those responsible for academic standards rapidly become well informed of the potential of such methods of delivery and the forms of assessment that may be appropriate. This will undoubtedly necessitate staff development for some senior academics, a notion that some may find distasteful. Further it becomes essential that the validation process has a suitable protocol built in whereby the student experience and academic rigour may be tested without imposing unreasonable restrictions on the course design team.

Guideline 3, Precept 14

Learning, although at a distance, should be treated as an activity involving all participants in the system, in which monitoring, review and feedback to those who manage the programmes of study are used regularly to enhance all components of teaching, learning and the system of delivery.

This clearly puts an onus on providing institutions and their programme or course directors to establish an effective ongoing process of continuous review and to act on the findings of such reviews to improve the overall delivery, management and administration of the programme. Virtually every institution has in place, on paper, such review mechanisms for traditional learning programmes. Experience suggests that many problems identified, by traditional review processes, are perennial in nature and have practical solutions that are not implemented because frequently the suggested remedies cross boundaries of the internal hierarchies of academia and administration. The clear requirement, namely to put in place effective mechanisms which will ensure that recommendations are carried forward to successful implementation, can only be met if the current *laissez-faire* culture is changed.

Guideline 5, Precept 16

A providing institution should meet the need of its students who are studying at a distance for information that is particularly full and clear about . . . the characteristics of the distance learning system and how students interact with it.

This precept clearly requires some wide-ranging explanations of how the programme will be run, what technology will be used, the methods of contact and support to be used and what is expected of the students. At the very least this requires a well-documented course handbook, at best perhaps a major programme of induction. Institutions may perhaps achieve this by incorporating such information into the validation protocols. This should not be onerous but perhaps may be of major cultural significance to those academics who are less than meticulous in their course introductions. Such a protocol will also help ensure that appropriate technology is employed rather than that which is readily available. ICT-based materials may be important elements within a course and if they assist 'A providing institution [should] meet the need of its students who are studying', and it should be immaterial whether they are part of a traditional or distance learning programme.

Guideline 5, Precept 17

A providing institution should monitor the effectiveness of information provided to students and, in the light of its findings, take steps to enhance its provision.

This precept will require similar actions to those in Guideline 3, Precept 14. This is in reality a requirement to audit and obtain student feedback on the course documentation, and to implement change as a result of the audit process. This is surely something that should happen in the management of traditional delivery, but which is often overtaken by lethargy and is therefore ineffective in moving programmes forward. Positive management action will again be necessary to change such attitudes.

Guideline 5, Precept 18

An institution should determine what means of student representation are appropriate and realistic for students on distance learning programmes of study and should provide these students with accurate information about them.

It is clear that, without being prescriptive, this precept looks for the establishment of practical and effective rather than complex processes of student representation. This will pose challenges for academics and administrators alike as they endeavour to design robust effective processes where perhaps none exist in support of current traditional programmes.

Guideline 6, Precept 19, Guideline 6, Precept 22 and Guideline 6, Precept 23

> A providing institution should be able to demonstrate publicly that summative assessment procedures . . . are appropriate for the mode of study . . . for the circumstances in which the programmes are studied.

And

> A providing institution should employ formative assessment as part of the design of distance learning programmes of study.

And

> A providing institution should monitor systematically the soundness of its assessment procedures and practice and be ready to amend them in the light of feedback.

These three precepts address the whole question of assessment, and alone should spark off significant debate not only in staff teams involved in course design but also among those charged with quality assurance. There will need to be fine judgements as to what constitutes distance learning, in the context of (some) elements of ICT-based materials being used in a traditional programme. Will it be necessary to apply these precepts? Who decides what forms of assessment are appropriate in the context of a module or course? Are the current controls on traditional programmes able to meet such potentially rigorous guidelines? Suffice it to say that this area will cause much friction between those rooted in traditional methods of assessment and those who hold more progressive views. As yet, many staff – both academic and administrative – are unaware of the possibilities of using a combination of formative and summative assessment. Staff training and development will become a minimum requirement, yet alone this will not be adequate.

There is a requirement to gather feedback about the assessment processes. But from whom? Students? External examiners? Academic standards staff? What are sound assessment processes? Who will define soundness? If we bring in new processes for ICT-based materials and distance learning, should the institutions adopt such criteria for traditionally delivered programmes?

Determination of these issues will require establishment of institutional working parties embracing subject specialists, student administrators and academic standards specialists, and those policy-makers responsible for academic matters. Such working groups will need to establish relevant measurement criteria for different programmes; which issues are unique to particular programmes and which common to all. They will need to implement measures to establish whether variations in recorded performance over time are measures of student variability, tutor variance, or diminishing relevance to workplace practices. These are not simple issues. The requirement to amend assessment processes when necessary means that the monitoring processes must be robust yet trigger change when necessary and then review the changes made.

MANAGING THE CHANGE, SOME OF THE ISSUES

To accommodate the changes presaged by the guidelines, institutions will need to manage the process of institutional change both operational and cultural.

Some students will be more comfortable and empowered by the new technologies; others will feel just the opposite. The removal of the need to attend at a fixed time and location will give more flexible use of time, but will require a different sort of motivation. Regular logging on to some form of conference area will become the norm; written contributions to discussion will be a key part of the learning process, and more modules will move to combinations of formative and summative assessment. Reflective writing will perhaps be more encouraged at lower levels than at present. Over time students will become more familiar and comfortable with exploratory learning, and didactic teaching will perhaps seem old-fashioned. Other students will welcome some chalk and talk as more familiar.

There will be both losers and gainers; the jury will be out for many years on which group will predominate. The only certainty is that technology will change for ever the way in which students learn and the way in which education is delivered and administered.

Institutions will need to initiate major programmes of staff development. Staff will need to become familiar with the current theories on learning and teaching and how the change from objectives to outcomes inevitably moves assessment from measuring inputs to assessing the ability of students to analyse, synthesise and problem-solve. Learning, perhaps, will be less about remembering information and more about applying generic tools to specific real situations or case studies. These moves will mean staff rethinking the content of their modules, and course directors and others questioning whether the historic approach to a subject or topic is any longer valid.

Staff will have to learn the capabilities and limitations of the new technologies. The technologies employed on the Internet are now advancing so rapidly that it is difficult to envisage whether academic staff will actually have the time to become technically competent and then keep up to date. There is a case for staff specifying what they want to use in their course material – text, animated slides, audio, video, webcam, online interaction, links to third party sites and so on – and then leaving the realisation of such specifications to fully trained educational technicians, thus freeing up comparatively highly paid staff to research and develop subject expertise and devise new and interesting strategies for enhancing the student experience. In some institutions there is already wide-ranging discussion of the desirability of every member of staff becoming competent with the new software packages. Will it, in fact, be feasible, when many are not yet competent on the existing packages, which are being continuously enhanced and at an accelerating rate? Institutions will need to decide whether, in the short term, academic staff should concentrate on the pedagogy and leave the application of the technology to specialists or whether to put in place programmes to train staff in the technologies.

CONCLUSIONS

Already in the progressive institutions there is significant argument among academics, administrators and senior directing staff about the policies, strategies and timings for embracing the new paradigms that use ICT. Different institutions are piloting different strategies and actively researching this large area of change, in the hope of being informed by best practice. It is already clear that there will be no one best method, yet the search for the Holy Grail continues. A range of options will emerge. Institutions will have to evaluate and make value judgements dependent on the target market and the subject area.

The institutional implications are widespread. Institutions will be required to take a managerially focused and holistic approach to meet the requirements of the QAA. It will be very difficult to satisfy Guideline 1, Precept 3 without a pan-institutional approach. Every course offered that uses ICT-based materials will require different technologies and teaching strategies. Each will place different demands on bodies such as quality assurance committees. Different administrative support and certainly different technical support will be a *sine qua non*. Staff training and development policy will need to recognise the need for these changed skills.

Decisions will have to be made about how technical support will be delivered and budgeted. Should it be centrally delivered as a top-sliced service or be provided and budgeted at school level? If centrally delivered, who will ensure that the level of support is adequate to meet the academic requirements?

Will institutions be able to support servers on a twenty-four-hours-a-day, seven-days-a-week basis including holiday periods based around Christian holy days, while recognising the multi-faith nature of society? Traditional work hours start to become meaningless. The notion of contact hours needs a complete rethink. Student attendance becomes very problematic. Internet-delivered courses are accessed at the convenience of the learner, not of the institution, but how can these long hours be adequately serviced? As institutions move to enrolling students from distant time zones the question of twenty-four-hour opening will become more critical.

As staff become more computer literate institutional policies will need to address issues such as staff accessibility to email and university management and information systems from remote locations. Individual web space on university computers will need to be available in support of teaching, research and publication. Those responsible for ICT services become nervous about such access since they dislike individual members of staff using file transfer to and from their workplace computers, yet this will need to be the norm when we move to twenty-four-hour support of distant students. Staff will need to be supported with provision of software for their use at home, at the same level as the in-institution provision. Provision of laptop computers or similar would be a way round this, but it does not solve the remote access problem.

It is inevitable that institutional policies, strategies and processes will have to change fundamentally to meet emerging distance learning benchmarks. The process of change will have to be continuous so as to keep pace with the advances in technology and meet current best practice. Start planning to manage that change now!

REFERENCES

Barr, Robert B. (1994) A Learning Paradigm for Colleges, California Association for Institutional Research – 1994 Annual Meeting 'Calls for Accountability: A Professional Response in a Political Environment'. San Diego, CA, 3–4 November. Available from http://www.cair.org/conferences/CAIR94/barr.html (accessed March 2003).

Quality Assurance Agency for Higher Education (QAA) (1999) *Guidelines for the Quality Assurance of Distance Learning.* QAA, Cheltenham. Available from http://www.qaa.ac.uk/public/dlg/contents.htm (accessed March 2003).

5

Building quality into ICT-based distance education

Marc Griffiths

INTRODUCTION

The present educational environment at the H. Lavity Stoutt Community College (HLSCC) may be described as teacher-centred. Most instructors adopt a 'blame the student' approach as described by Biggs (1999). The teaching and learning activities that are used in the classroom are largely 'traditional'. Lectures are the predominant means of delivering content. An increasing number of technological tools are in place around the college, and one of the institution's goals is to have instructors use this technology more effectively in the teaching and learning process. As a part of the drive to incorporate technology into education, the college is looking to leverage its existing technology infrastructure to implement a web-based distance education system that is suited to the college's unusual geographical circumstances. The new venture must provide a quality of learning that is equivalent to or better than that of the face-to-face classroom.

THE BRITISH VIRGIN ISLANDS

The HLSCC was founded in 1990 and is the British Virgin Islands' (BVI) only tertiary-level institution. The British Virgin Islands (which remains a British colony) is a group of about fifty small islands located in the northern Caribbean just east of Puerto Rico. Currently, HLSCC has two physical campuses located in the two main population centres in the group of islands. The main campus is located on Tortola, the biggest of the islands in the BVI, and the satellite campus is located on Virgin Gorda, the island with the second largest population.

The total population of the BVI is around 20,000. About half of the BVI's population is considered to be expatriates. The majority of these expatriates come from the surrounding Caribbean region, North America and Europe. The BVI's popularity results from the strength of its economy (one of the strongest in the region) and the use of the US dollar as its official currency. The two pillars of the BVI economy are the financial services and tourism industries. Tourism currently accounts for about 45 per cent of national income. The financial services industry generates substantial revenues through incorporation fees charged to companies registering in the territory. According to the BVI Financial Services website there are an estimated 400,000 companies registered in the BVI. These two industries attract professionals from all over the world to the shores of the BVI. The BVI population represents a diverse mix of culture and ethnicity. This mix is represented in the student body, staff and faculty of HLSCC. Apart from cultural and ethnic diversity, the students at HLSCC reflect significant differences in age (minimum age 16), educational background and experience.

H. LAVITY STOUTT COMMUNITY COLLEGE

In accordance with its mission, HLSCC offers courses and programmes designed to enable a smooth transition from the college into upper-level courses at universities and colleges. HLSCC has a number of formal articulation agreements with US colleges, which enable students to transfer seamlessly from the college into the second or third year of a Bachelors programme at those schools. Most other US schools evaluate HLSCC students on a case-by-case basis. The principal tools used in the evaluation process are the course outlines that specify the content and learning outcomes for the course and the students' transcripts that show how the students performed in the courses. The need to provide students with the ability to transfer directly into US universities and colleges has a dramatic impact on the design of the college's courses. In addition, the college offers courses that prepare students to take the Cambridge Advanced Level (A Level) examinations and/or the Caribbean Advanced Proficiency Examination (CAPE). The A Levels and CAPE serve primarily as the entry requirements for students who wish to attend the University of the West Indies (UWI) or others in the UK or Canada. The A Levels are being phased out, and will be replaced by the regionally developed and managed CAPE, dubbed the Caribbean A Levels. CAPE is designed to serve primarily as matriculation to UWI. Only time will tell if CAPE can achieve universal acceptance at schools outside of the Caribbean region. The Caribbean Examination Council (CXC), the organisation that manages CAPE, does have a history as an examining body, and the ordinary-level equivalent exams have been accepted outside of the region for many years.

The college is organised along the lines of community colleges found in the USA. The college operates on a semester system. The academic year starts in August and ends in July. Each academic year comprises three semesters (autumn, spring, summer). The spring and autumn semesters are seventeen weeks long (including holidays and examinations) and the summer semester is six weeks in duration. Student enrolment at the college each semester is approximately 750 students (fewer in summer).

The majority of students enrolled at the college attend part time. The college accommodates the requirements of its entire student body by offering courses from 8:30 a.m. to 9:00 p.m. Monday to Thursday, 8:30 a.m. to 12:00 noon on Friday and 9:00 a.m. to 12:00 noon on Saturday. As a rule a course meets for three to four hours each week.

A goal of HLSCC is to provide access to tertiary-level education to the entire population of the territory. Currently, only students who can attend courses at the main campus on Tortola have access to the full range of programmes and courses offered by the college. The small campus on Virgin Gorda offers students access to a limited number of programmes and courses. Only certificate of achievement programmes are offered at the Virgin Gorda campus. Students on all the other islands within the BVI must commute to one of the campuses to take courses. The limited schedule operated by the ferry services between the islands makes commuting difficult. As a result, students on the other islands must move to Tortola to attend the college. For some students this option is not suitable for a variety of reasons. It should be noted that the college does not provide any student accommodation.

Approximately, seventy-five full-time and adjunct faculty are employed to cover the range of times and the number of courses required to meet the demands of the student body. Each semester it is necessary to schedule several sections of the most popular courses to satisfy the demand. Even though multiple sections of a course are scheduled at different times during the day, and on different days of the week, some students find that they are unable to enrol on the courses they need. Part-time students especially find it difficult when the times of course offerings conflict with other commitments or clash with other required courses. The difficulty may be a result of their being unable to gain their employer's consent to take courses at the scheduled times, the shifts they work conflicting with the times of the course, religious observance or other personal commitments. This problem is often compounded for some students by the registration process. The college registers students on a first-come-first-served basis. Students are often frustrated when they try to register and find that the courses they require are full. This is especially true of the general education courses required by the majority of students.

The physical restrictions experienced by the college (number of classrooms, labs, number of faculty, classroom size) mean that the college has no immediate solution to the problems faced by the student body. The implementation of web-based distance education is seen as a possible solution to some of the frustrations being experienced by students. Web-based distance education is also seen as a way to extend the influence of the college beyond the boundaries of the BVI, and to provide marketing opportunities both in the Caribbean region and the wider world.

The teaching environment

The growing call within the institution for the use of technology in the classroom has led to the increased use of standard software tools such as Microsoft PowerPoint. HLSCC possesses a wealth of technology which may be exploited in the classroom. There is a campus-wide computer network. Each member of faculty is equipped with a computer that is connected to the network. Students have access to the network via four fully equipped computer labs. Wireless access points in place around the campus provide access to the network from any location on the campus. Via the network, Faculty and students have access to the Internet and a wide range of productivity tools. The existing technologies provide excellent opportunities for integrating technology into the classroom. However, it may be argued that the way in which the technology is used has not improved either the quality of education provided or the experience for the student.

The use of technology so far has caused only minor improvements (in some cases) in the educational experiences of the students. The technology is often used as an electronic blackboard. In education, computers should be used as a tool to represent knowledge and not simply as a vehicle for the dissemination of information. In many institutions the computer is used all too often as an electronic blackboard. This limitation in thinking about how technology is implemented in the teaching and learning process limits the impact that technology can have on the quality of education. It is suggested that technology can achieve its greatest impact in education when it is implemented as a 'mindtool' (Jonassen *et al.*, 1998): 'Mindtools are cognitive reflection and amplification tools that help learners to construct their own realities by designing their own knowledge bases.' The question then remains: How can technology be implemented in the classroom in such a way that it improves both the quality of education and the student experience?

The teaching process

This section focuses on the teaching processes as they occur within the Computer Studies Department. The lecturers in the Computer Studies Department are untrained teachers with limited teaching experience. This situation is generally representative of all the departments.

At the start of each course the lecturer provides students with a copy of the course outline (syllabus). The course outline gives a detailed description of the course content and learning objectives for the course. The course outline is especially important when multiple sections of a course are taught in a semester by different lecturers, since a common final is given. Based on the content specified in the course outline, lecturers prepare activities for the courses they teach. The most commonly used activity in the classroom is the lecture. During lectures students are expected to take notes. The notes are often dictated, or in some cases students must decide what they consider important enough to note during the lecture.

To satisfy the demand of the administration to use more technology in the classroom, lecturers have started to incorporate the use of LCD projectors and Microsoft PowerPoint presentations into their lectures. These tools have allowed lecturers to prepare very flashy presentations for their classes. These electronic presentations have added little value to the classroom experience, since they are used as electronic blackboards. Even with the technology the students must still take notes. The only difference is that it is probably easier for students than having the notes dictated or placed on the blackboard. This shows that the technology has not changed the classroom experience of the students. Technology may be used to present a lecture more effectively, and if students are provided with the notes, then more meaningful (useful) learning activities may be planned for the classroom. Observations suggest that students are not given the lecture notes since note-taking is the primary teaching/learning activity for many lecturers. For these lecturers, if students have access to the notes then there is little need for them to attend class. The course content is now at the students' fingertips. Why then should they attend a lecture where the same content will be read to them, when they can now read it at their convenience?

The above description demonstrates note-taking as the primary learning activity in the classroom. It also suggests a teaching philosophy based on the idea that students are empty vessels waiting to be filled with information. Experience demonstrates that once students have access to the notes they use the lecture time to engage in activities which they find more interesting. Computer courses at the college are taught in a computer laboratory, and students have been observed happily using the instant messaging programs, surfing the web and typing their homework as the notes are read to them.

Clearly, current classroom activities are ineffective at engaging students. Through informal discussions with colleagues and students and reflecting on my own practices, I have concluded that most of us realise at some level that some of our classroom activities are ineffective. I draw this conclusion because most colleagues whom I spoke to had advice or techniques for trying to increase student involvement in the note-taking/reading activities. Two common approaches to solving the problem seem to exist. The first was to prevent the students from having access to computers during the lecture. This is easily achieved by using software that locks each computer in the lab from the instructor's console. However, this results in students having nothing to do, so they simply look bored as the notes are read to them. The second approach involves leaving blank slides (sections) in the notes that would be 'discussed' and filled in during class. The idea here is that students will pay attention to ensure they get all of the notes. After all, notes are a record of what has been covered in the classroom that must be learned and reproduced on assessments in the future.

Another common thread in the discussions revolved around our own experiences as students. The suggestion is that the approach worked for us as students, so it must be effective. This means that the problem lies not with our methods but with the students. A lack of motivation on the part of the student is suggested as one of the greatest hurdles we face as instructors. The elusive characteristic motivation that seems to determine success needs to be addressed. Students need to be motivated is often the cry. The question is: How do we motivate students not to be bored during a lecture? The suggestion is to get them to understand the importance of what we are doing in class and of education as a whole. After all, if the students are told that their futures depend on it they will be motivated. Motivation is accepted as a component necessary for success, and this approach does work for some students. However, sustaining this type of motivation for the duration of the programme is difficult.

TEACHING FOR QUALITY

The literature provides valuable insights about teaching methods; many authors suggest different ways in which technology may be used more effectively in teaching (see e.g. Laurillard, 1993). However, Biggs (1998, 1999) suggests that perhaps it is not simply the students and their attitudes that need investigation, but the overall teaching philosophy: 'When students don't learn (that is, when teaching breaks down), it is due to something the students are lacking.'

It is often suggested that 'good' students will learn in spite of what we do to them. The real challenge is getting the 'average' and 'poor' students to perform (behave) like good students. We are therefore challenged to adopt a new approach to teaching and learning. This means abandoning the old philosophy that it worked for me as a student and replacing it with a new philosophy that it is 'what the student does' and not the teacher that is important.

> If students are to learn desired outcomes in a reasonably effective manner, then the teacher's fundamental task is to get students to engage in learning activities that are likely to result in their achieving those outcomes. It is helpful to remember that what the student does is actually more important in determining what is learned than what the teacher does.
>
> (Thomas J. Shuell, 1986, quoted by Biggs, 1999)

An enhanced teaching system based on the principle of 'constructive alignment' aims to align the desired objectives with the teaching and learning activities best suited to achieve them and the assessment which demonstrates that the required outcomes have been achieved. Such aligned assessment serves a double purpose: it checks the quality of learning, and for students, it defines what is to be learned.

In developing the web-based distance education course the decision was made to build quality into the online courses from the very beginning. Constructive alignment is used as the underlying principle to ensure quality in all of the course offerings. The course objectives were revisited and reworded as verbs which the students would be able to demonstrate. Teaching and learning activities are being developed that allow students to enact the verbs specified in the objectives. New assessment methods are being designed that enable students to demonstrate that they have attained the desired level of learning. The principle of constructive alignment seems to fit the goals of the project well, one of which is to use technology to encourage a deep learning approach (Duffy and Jonassen, 1992).

It is hoped that apart from providing improved accessibility and convenience to the students of the territory, the web-based distance education system will influence the way in which courses are designed and delivered to students. The quality of learning can be enhanced through this medium by adopting a more student-centred approach. Through the development of course material that is designed to fit the local context and to be sensitive to the experiences of local students, the new approach should engage students more in their learning activities and promote the development of confidence and higher order thinking skills. However, in doing this the differences that exist between the local community and the wider global community should not be neglected. Students at the college are required in a changing global environment to be cognisant of the differences that exist, and must be prepared to interact and function within the global community. The BVI's population is multicultural with approximately half the population expatriate. The educational system within the territory must be prepared to handle this.

Technology should be used as a tool to enhance the experience and quality of learning of students. As Staley and Mackenzie (2000) state, '[U]nfortunately, many examples to date indicate a more common approach is to simply automate existing curricula and re-inforce learning processes that have existed for centuries.'

Jonassen *et al.* (1998) suggest five roles for technology in the learning process:

1   to represent learners' ideas;
2   to provide access to the information necessary for knowledge construction (multiple perspectives);
3   to provide a real world context that can support learning by doing;
4   to act as a tool for collaboration between learners;
5   to serve as intellectual partners that support reflection on the tasks being performed.

Incorporating technology into the roles suggested would help to move the technology away from being simply a presentation tool and into the realm of a tool capable of assisting students in the learning process. A 'constructivist learning environment' (CLE) would be ideally suited to the online courses since students would be provided with a complete environment in which they can interact, explore and learn.

One aim of developing an online learning environment at HLSCC is to provide greater access to college for the students within the territory. The provision should offer students the flexibility of being able to enrol on the college courses regardless of their location within the territory or the time at which the courses are offered. Online education should free the students from the shackles of classroom learning.

The development of a CLE gives the opportunity to evaluate a new delivery system which may prove that it can enhance the quality of the education provided, by encouraging students to be more independent, active and to enhance their critical thinking skills. Overall the project will provide an institution-wide framework for the development and delivery of online courses. This framework will be used to investigate the impact on the student in terms of its cultural implications and learning outcomes and its impact on teaching approaches.

In order to support the five roles of technology within the context of an online constructivist learning environment the course will be set up to provide students with:

- problem space;
- related cases;
- information sources;
- knowledge construction tools;
- conversational tools (communication tools).

The online delivery system has been piloted with the CSC 113 Programming Language 1 course. This is an introductory programming course which introduces students to problem-solving using an object-oriented methodology and the C++ programming language. This course is viewed as an ideal course to pilot since the students enrolled on this course would have attended at least one semester at the college, and all of the students enrolled on this course will be majors in either the Associate Degree or Certificate of Higher Education in Computer Studies. This means that all of the students enrolled should possess basic computer skills, including the use of the Internet. This will hopefully help the course to progress quite smoothly because of the initial computing experience. CSC 113 is the second of three programming courses in the programme. The students would have already been introduced to solving computer-based problems and would have written simple programs using Visual Basic. None of the students are expected to have any prior experience with this form of distance education.

CONCEPTUALISATION

The Kolb learning cycle as interpreted by Staley and MacKenzie (2000) was used to visualise how technology may be applied in the programming course at each stage of the cycle. Since this course will be offered entirely online, the technology must be used to support each stage (conceptualisation, planning, experience and reflection) of the cycle.

Conceptualisation deals with the knowledge base required to perform the activities in the course. In terms of thinking about conceptualisation, the level and experience of the students is important. The conceptualisation stage will be implemented as the information source for the course. While most of the students would have completed at least one semester of college work, it is expected that most will need to be provided with structure and guidance as to the content to be covered. The course outline will be used to provide the overall structure for content to be acquired. Each objective will be linked to relevant notes and references where the students will be able to find the information required. In addition, students will be given credit for providing additional resources that may be used by other students in the course. This will help to encourage cooperation among students through the sharing of resources (McConnell, 2000).

People cooperate for three reasons:

1 for external reward;
2 to form and further relationships;
3 to share the activities they are involved in.

Cooperation in the classroom is presently not the norm, so it is felt that an additional incentive is needed to foster the cooperative spirit in students. Deadlines must be imposed on the learning activities to keep the course moving forward. While the online environment provides learners with a great deal of autonomy, it is anticipated that the inexperience of our students with this form of learning will require a more formal structure to assist them with the time management requirements of the course. This is particularly important when taking into account that one of the constraints we face is that the course must be completed within the fifteen-week semester in which it is offered. Staley and MacKenzie (2000) acknowledge this need for more structure for some groups of students:

> Increasing student autonomy, and developing 'learning to learn' skills is very laudable, although some less motivated students and certainly many of the instrumental students will require considerable help and support.

It is expected that a wide variety of students will enrol on this course; however, none are expected have experienced working in a programming environment. This means that a lot of the concepts to be learned will be abstract to the students. It is important that the learning environment provides a mechanism that allows students to consider how these concepts may be applied to everyday situations and industries. One activity associated with the objectives is a report that requires students to think about the way in which the concepts may be applied in their home, work or academic lives. These reports require students to provide a concrete real-life situation that demonstrates how they can apply the concepts they are learning to everyday situations. These reports will hopefully provide a rich resource that enables the entire class to appreciate different contexts in which programming can be implemented. This, along with examples provided by the instructor, will form the related cases needed for students to appreciate the different contexts in which the course content may be applied. The added benefit of this type of activity is that it may be extended into the realm of experience if students are able to implement their ideas and produce programming products based on the ideas. This may not always be possible depending on the level of complexity of the problems identified. It is envisioned that online discussions (synchronous and asynchronous) will provide the medium for the sharing and critiquing of ideas and products. We feel that this is particularly important as we try to develop in our students the ability to think critically about their learning and not merely to passively absorb information.

The existing technology may be used to provide students with concrete experiences of what they are learning and why. The constructivist learning environment will support this through the problem space. Projects will be designed to simulate a real-world programming environment. In the problem space the students will interact and solve real-world situations related to programming. The plan is to present case studies using multimedia elements for the students to solve in groups. We view group activities as a crucial part of the programming curriculum since most real programming projects are solved by groups of programmers working together on a problem. It is hoped that the technology may be used to simulate situations such as communications breakdowns, disagreements among group members and misunderstandings of requirements. The related cases will present the students with examples of what can be done with the subject matter being learned. This will provide students with examples of how the content can be transferred and implemented in different contexts.

The virtual experiences will be supported by discussions in two ways. First, the students or groups will be required to discuss how they intend to solve the problem (apply theory to practice), and indicate why they think their approach would be successful (reflection). Second, the students will implement their solution (construction) and check the results to test if it matched their expectations. A report outlining any differences between results and expectations would be produced. Differences will be explained and alternative solutions suggested where appropriate. This should promote reflection on the activities performed and would require students to think about how they apply their conceptual knowledge in the production of the solution. It will be ideal if the students are able to solve many different problems situated in different contexts. The time constraints of the course may make this impractical. However, it is hoped that the database of related cases plus the different problems undertaken by the individual students can be developed as a rich resource that enables the students to at least read (and hopefully see) how the same knowledge may be applied in different contexts, the types of problems encountered and solutions to those problems.

As stated above, the course outline will be used to provide the structure for the content of the course. Students will be encouraged to use the outline as the starting point for their investigation into the subject matter. Links to other relevant resources will be provided to help guide students to further information on the subject matter, and students will be encouraged (rewarded) for sharing additional resources with the rest of the class. This will hopefully both help to promote collaboration and demonstrate the importance attached to going beyond the information given.

Programming is an ideal subject to implement in a CLE; the nature of programming forces students to apply conceptual knowledge all the time in the construction of programs (Ben-Ari, 2001). The integrated development environment (IDE) provides an ideal knowledge representation tool that gives students rapid feedback as to the success or failure of the assumptions they are testing. Students learn programming by actively exploring the language and testing assumptions in the IDE. The real challenge here is to try to promote reflection. It is possible that students engage in these activities without thinking about why the environment responded in the way that it did. They can be lulled into randomly trying different combinations until they find something that works.

These are just some of the activities that are planned to use technology in support of learning outcomes in developing the web-based course at HLSCC. Other activities being considered include 'pair programming' described by Williams and Upchurch (2001) and 'explorations' described by Lischner (2001).

SUMMARY

The results of this project will not be known for some time. If successful the results will be used to inform the design and development of an online programme that can be offered throughout the Caribbean region.

From the outset of this project the goal has been to provide as complete a learning environment online for the students as possible. The environment is designed to use technology to support the learning outcomes. The quality of the online education must at least be equivalent to the face-to-face classroom. To achieve this we have considered our student population, our teaching and learning philosophies and our outcomes, and from this we have devised an approach that we feel will provide the quality of education desired. This approach considered from the very beginning how the technology would be implemented to support the quality of learning desired.

It was decided at the beginning that the approach we would use would not merely transfer our methods, content and approaches used in the classroom to the online environment. We also wanted to develop at our institution an educational system tailored to the needs and expectations of our population, and one which uses methods that will enhance the quality of the learning experience.

REFERENCES

Ben-Ari, M. (2001) Constructivism in computer science education. *Journal of Computers in Mathematics and Science Teaching* 20 (1): 45–73.

Biggs, J. (1998) What the student does: teaching for enhanced learning in the '90s. HERDA Conference Proceedings. Available from www2.Auckland.ac.uk/cpd/HERDSA/HTML/TchLearn/Biggs1.htm (accessed February 2004).

Biggs, J. (1999) *Teaching for Quality Learning at University*. Buckingham: Society for Research into Higher Education and Open University Press.

Duffy, T.M. and Jonassen, D. (1992) *Constructivism and the Technology of Instruction: A Conversation*. Hillsdale, NJ: Lawrence Erlbaum Associates.

Jonassen, D., Peck, K.L., Wilson, B.G. and Pfeiffer, W.S. (1998) *Learning with Technology: A Constructivist Perspective*. Upper Saddle River, NJ: Prentice Hall.

Laurillard, D. (1993) *Rethinking University Teaching: A Framework for the Effective Use of Educational Technology*. London: Routledge.

Lischner, R. (2001) *Explorations: Structured Labs for First-time Programmers*. Proceedings of SIGCSE 2001 Conference. Charlotte: ACM Press, pp. 154–8.

McConnell, D. (2000) *Implementing Computer Supported Cooperative Learning*. London: Kogan Page.

Staley, A. and MacKenzie, A. (2000) Enabling curriculum re-design through asynchronous learning networks. *Journal of Asynchronous Learning Networks*. Available from http://www.aln.org/alnweb/journal/Vol4_issue1/staley MacKenzie.htm (accessed February 2004).

Williams, L. and Upchurch, R. (2001) In support of student pair-programming. Available from http://pairprogramming.com/WilliamsUpchurch.pdf (accessed February 2004).

6

Unlocking key barriers for staff on the path to an e-University

Gillian Jordan and Jill Jameson

SUMMARY

This case study identifies key barriers for staff on the path of development from a conventional campus university into a model of delivery based upon ICT – an e-University – and suggests ways to unlock these barriers. The focus of this evidence-based research is an e-University pilot development in virtual learning in progress at the University of Greenwich. Documentary evidence for the study included feedback from twelve sub-projects in the overall e-University development designed to test 'fitness for purpose' in delivering an M.Sc. e-Commerce degree programme. Written commentary from staff on the steering group and from professional external facilitators PricewaterhouseCoopers on business modelling provided evidence of key barriers and suggestions on ways to overcome them. The authors took as their guiding principle a main focus on delivering excellence in learning for students. To recommend successful methods of unlocking the main barriers for staff on the path to an institutional implementation of e-learning, an 'e-University Key Barrier Matrix' was developed.

BACKGROUND

In the current global stampede to convert courses for web-based delivery, the identification and unlocking of key barriers to successful whole-institution implementation of e-learning is possibly the single most important competitive advantage a university can possess. In this short chapter, we deal with this issue in relation, in particular, to staffing issues. The focus on 'barriers for staff' is deliberate, in recognition of the 'make-or-break' significance which staff at a range of levels can have in the institutional change processes involved in introducing e-learning (Hall, 2001). The locus of our study is the University of Greenwich – a UK regional university for Southeast London and Kent, with a number of areas of international expertise, and a main campus situated at the historic Wren-designed Royal Naval College site in Maritime Greenwich.

With almost 18,000 students on undergraduate and postgraduate programmes, the University has responded to emerging demographic trends of student study–work combinations by widening its range of part-time and flexible study routes.

Initially, e-learning initiatives have been developed, innovation-driven by expert staff enthusiasts, but, more recently, steps have been taken to move the approach into the mainstream. Pilot project funding from the Higher Education Funding Council for England, combined with funding for strategic learning and teaching initiatives, enabled a range of developments to take place at the University of Greenwich.

To integrate e-learning into the University, and rethink students' learning in terms of e-facilities as recommended by previous researchers (Laurillard, 1993), the Greenwich e-U project was conceptualised in relation to the University's Framework for Learning (Humphreys, 1998). In this Framework, learning has been envisaged in terms of a number of generic delivery functions (University of Greenwich, 2000). Twelve e-University sub-projects were mapped against these delivery functions to act as a test bed for the University's capability to support learning using facilities, resources and services for electronic delivery through a pilot Master's degree programme – an M.Sc. e-Commerce – to be delivered 100 per cent online. All aspects of e-learning delivery are being tested and evaluated for 'fitness of purpose', so that e-delivery of each separate facility may, once 'fit', be applied selectively to a range of mainstream degree programmes. The sub-projects cover all aspects of learning and related support infrastructure. Each sub-project has a clearly stated aim with related tasks and is led by a member of academic, technical or administrative staff with expertise in the sub-project area (ibid.). The outcome overall will be the delivery and evaluation of the M.Sc. and the selected mainstreaming of the sub-projects.

METHOD OF IDENTIFYING KEY BARRIERS ON THE PATH

In travelling the e-University development path, we have encountered specific barriers to progress that are particularly important for staff. We have found it useful to identify these barriers, prioritise those that are key to success, and seek a range of ways of overcoming these barriers.

Evidence-based research in the form of a descriptive case study (Yin, 1994) may be a helpful way of enabling an institution to examine the implementation of innovations in learning and teaching, with the aim of developing good practice. Our identification of key barriers for staff and recommendations for the resolution of problems connected with implementing this kind of 'borderless education' is informed by prior work on the subject of e-learning (CVCP, 2000). We recognise that these obstacles are not unique to us. However, we anticipate that sharing local perceptions of e-barriers and ways round them with a larger audience will be a valuable and relevant exercise for us all as we engage in dialogue and exchange of experiences in the implementation of virtual learning. In identifying barriers to progress, written evidence from the steering group for the project, and the report of an external facilitator from PricewaterhouseCoopers (Block *et al.*, 2001), were used. A range of problems was identified from the examination of these sources. These may be grouped under the general headings of institutional distractions, leadership and skills issues, e-critics, communications and overload problems, and quality barriers for staff.

KEY BARRIERS IDENTIFIED

Key Barrier 1 – Institutional distractions

At the time of implementation of this virtual learning project, the University was undergoing a major restructuring programme. This change was perceived by the e-University steering group as a potential distraction. A general institutional focus on restructuring drew some staff away from the aims of the Greenwich e-U project. A number of staff due to complete sub-projects were pulled out to complete important work needed for restructuring. The 'hard data' perceived as necessary by the external facilitator for business modelling were not forthcoming by the specified date, staff were forced to cancel meetings, and were unable to carry out work as originally agreed.

A tendency to marginalise the virtual learning project occurred through these distractions. Staff regarded their main university work as more important and significant than the e-development. The perception by some academic heads of department that the virtual learning project was an unnecessary drain on staff time did not square with the investment in funding provided to release lecturing staff from other duties. Simultaneously, some unclarity arose about the perceived overall institutional aims of the virtual learning project. One staff member commented, 'I'm kind of confused about where we are and where we are going.' Different perceptions arose about the main focus of the e-University: a separate entity with its own name, market, staff and facilities, or a complementary enhancement to the mainstream activity of the University. Significant institutional distractions can arise in the implementation of virtual learning. This is more challenging in a situation complicated both by comprehensive institutional change and confusions in perceived aims.

Unlocking Barrier 1 – Stay motivated and keep your eye on the ball!
In our case, the knowledge that the e-University development will make a positive contribution to the University's new structure has been an incentive to continued motivation. The original specification of the project as a vehicle to test 'fitness for purpose' in virtual learning against the Framework for Learning had a useful degree of conceptual integrity for student learning. The guidance of managers to concentrate on 'keeping your eye on the ball' at a time of major institutional change was helpful in retaining staff motivation and steering the project through uncertainties. Staying motivated and focused on the original aims of the e-project therefore unlocks the first obstacle of institutional distractions.

Key Barrier 2 – Confused perceptions of leadership and decision-making

In terms of leadership, differences in understanding the remit of the project complicated decision-making, since a number of levels, strands of management and committee structures were involved. Swift decision-making was hence impeded, as recommendations for decisions suggested by the steering group for the project were not always in tune with the ideas of all, and a range of staff at different tiers in the University needed to know, understand and agree with the aims of the project. A variety of expertise in and enthusiasm for e-learning existed at different levels of management. Institutional recognition of who precisely was 'leading' the project was sometimes perceived as unclear, since there were 'leaders' at different levels in a somewhat extensive chain of command. Enthusiasts at a number of hierarchical levels were perceived by staff in the steering group to have a leading role in knowledge and experience, while others, more remote, might have actualised authority in terms of decision-making on, for example, finances. Such discrepancies could lead to delays, misunderstandings and confusion.

Surmounting these particular barriers has required a number of small forays into what Schön (1983) calls the 'swampy lowlands' in order to get back on to the main path. A major strength in this has been the existence of the twelve sub-projects (University of Greenwich, 2000). As each worked to a mini-business model, progress on individual projects made contributions to the whole. Sub-projects developed at varying speeds – when one area of development was behind schedule, another was demonstrating substantial advances. This assisted cross-fertilisation and transference of ideas and skills. Regular project meetings were essential to facilitate this process. Werner comments (Werner, 2001) that effective results from this kind of small-scale focused sub-project work are crucial – 'cultures change when pockets of people find success and the word spreads'.

A vital area for decision-making has been that of determining the appropriate virtual learning environment to be used in the e-University. The chosen platform had to provide electronic access to all relevant facilities, resources and services of the e-University and be compatible with existing hardware/software used by the University as a whole. One sub-project was briefed with the task of identifying a range of virtual learning environments (VLEs) and evaluating their relevance and usability. A major problem was that an initial decision was taken to adopt a particular commercial VLE for new developments, before the sub-project team had been able to evaluate a range of available platforms, while existing e-learning provision was using a different VLE. The solution to this has been to adopt an 'e-Toolkit' to test a variety of platforms. This has the disadvantage that in the short term more staff development and ongoing technical support have been needed, but the advantage that, if a decision is made to use only one platform, it will be a fully informed strategic decision arising from extensive evaluative comparisons across a range of possible platforms in the toolkit. The 'e-Toolkit' approach allows greater institutional accommodation of a variety of learning practices: this approach may be continued indefinitely if ongoing evaluation reveals that having only one platform is not the best institutional solution.

Unlocking Barrier 2 – Identify leadership, achieve consensus
In opening up this second barrier, it is helpful to all if clear leadership of an e-learning development is identified at a number of levels from the outset, and decision-making processes clarified and disseminated. As Hall notes (Hall, 2001), a steering committee involving a range of functional managers can be useful. Delegation of specific areas of decision-making can promote local ownership, while wide-ranging consultation is vital to ensure the sympathies and understandings of participants. This combination of clear leadership and effective consultation can achieve a growth in university-wide understanding and ownership of the role and purpose of e-University developments. Public support for the project from top university managers has been vital in this process.

Key Barrier 3 – Skills and staff development issues

The identification of staff who have appropriate skills for the implementation of a vehicle for testing 'fitness of purpose' of the University for e-learning was complicated by some lack of recognition of existing staff expertise. One learning and teaching developer commented, somewhat nostalgically,

> five years ago we were ahead of the field in the development of interactive collaborative learning on line . . . in planning any future e-University, we need to retain the raison d'être for e-support in its original form, i.e. to support learners who feel isolated . . . and retain and extend the expertise . . . goodwill and motivation of original developer/enthusiasts who are our e-University champions.
>
> (Block *et al.*, 2001)

The implementation of the project did not automatically achieve this, since the selection of staff did not initially draw on this original group of enthusiasts. Latterly, however, enthusiasts for e-learning were drawn in to use their expertise, as were new staff with unique and hitherto unused vital skills in instructional design and applications development. Both original and new staff with e-learning experience have acted as advisers and mentors to those developing the M.Sc. e-Commerce. In some ways this work highlighted as many problems as have been solved, since the pedagogical model for the M.Sc. e-Commerce has so far been predominantly a transmissive didactic one (Moll and Whitmore, 1993). The development team has focused more on translating lecture materials into web format than on using the potential of the web for creating a collaborative, peer-supported transactional learning environment (Jordan and Ryan, 1999). The pressure on the development team to prepare the programme for validation procedures has inevitably made staff somewhat resistant to embrace new or different models of learning, and the M.Sc. has initially had a teacher-centred format. The positive aspect of this is that the nature of web-delivered materials lends itself more readily to development than paper-based distance learning materials, and the team is keen to participate in activities aimed at facilitating ongoing and dynamic enhancements of the programme. Re-examining the nature of the learning experience itself remains a key focus in the management of the project, and one that has not been subject to confused perceptions. The core values of providing excellence in student learning, informed by models of e-learning student support (Jameson and Squires, 2000), has been a useful common denominator in ensuring staff commitment to skills development.

One recommendation of the Business Modelling Day (Block *et al.*, 2001) was that 'An organisational migration plan is required to implement this strategy as an enterprise-wide e-learning model'. A move to wider e-learning requires the involvement of more staff who need development to engage with the technological and pedagogical aspects of e-tutoring. Not all staff are interested in acquiring new skills, and many see e-learning as a threat to the status quo. This is a particular problem when a major restructuring threatens job security.

Unlocking Barrier 3 – Value and develop staff, identify and use expertise
To open up Barrier 3, a recognition that staff expertise and enthusiasm is a valuable commodity in the implementation of an e-project can be helpful. It is important to engage sympathies, involve staff, and ensure that training, mentoring and advice are available. Developing a more sophisticated pedagogical model for collaborative peer-supported interactive learning may be achieved through such processes. The recognition of core values can be a useful common denominator.

Key Barrier 4 – E-critics, communications and overload problems

Problems arose in working across all university schools. Perceptions of academics that the e-project was a potential threat to their futures echo the considerable effect that this 'major renegotiation of pedagogy and authority' (Faigley, 1998) – perhaps inevitably bound up with the introduction of online learning – is having globally. Just as environmental critics of the Internet argue that 'when our own communities have become unsafe, uncertain, unpleasant, and ugly, we seek artificial ones' (Faigley, 1998), so academic e-critics have argued that the nature of learning is, inevitably, negatively affected. A perceived diminution of educational integrity is regarded by some as a necessary downside to e-learning. To counter such criticism, which can arise from those with least experience of e-working, it is helpful to have excellent, regular communications and information dissemination on the developments involved, and to be effective in keeping to deadlines. Considerable difficulties can arise with workload to achieve this, however. Staff in this e-U project were seconded from full-time university jobs. Problems arose with staff workloads already very heavy with routine university work, and meeting deadlines was an ongoing problematic issue. This is a common issue in many work areas – staff with particular skills are often called upon to carry out additional duties. The solution will be that, in time, as specialist skills become more widely cascaded, more people will be available to meet the new demands.

Unlocking Barrier 4 – Communicate well, release staff from overload
To counter e-critics, good communication in 'frequent, specific messages' engaging staff in real conversations about acknowledged problems, and meeting deadlines effectively through 'high intensity participation', can be crucial (Werner, 2001). Cascading specialist skills and releasing specialist staff from mundane duties to enable concentrated e-development can free up overburdened staff and help the project succeed.

Key Barrier 5 – Quality problems which staff face

A major consideration in our thinking and development has been to ensure staff are supported with good-quality e-provision. Quality is an overarching concept referring not only to materials provided but also to all aspects of the learning experience, including student support, access to resources, technical back-up, and the match between pedagogical models, subject areas and students' entry abilities. Close attention to quality is important to safeguard staff and institutional reputations, although a cynic might suggest that the ultimate arbiter of quality will be the consumer. E-learning quality issues need to be monitored carefully. Just as pedagogical models do not necessarily transfer effectively from one mode of delivery to another, neither do quality assurance mechanisms. The focus has therefore been on the funding and development of quality standards and protocols for materials design, technical/web page specification, registration, and other critical processes – and specific related staff development. According to a CVCP study into the implications of global borderless education, 'for some time to come, borderless developments are likely to add significant complexity to the task of quality management at institutional, national and international levels' (CVCP, 2000). Some e-learning innovators feel that bespoke remodelling of existing quality assurance processes is over-rigorous and unfair to them, but the aim is to provide clear quality assurance checks (QAA, 1999), and to ensure that staff are supported and trained well.

Unlocking Barrier 5 – Concentrate on achieving quality – no shortcuts
The assurance of quality in content as well as in the general learning environment is essential for staff to achieve effective e-learning development. No shortcuts should be allowed in this process, or staff and institutional reputations will be at risk and customers will vote with their feet. Hence to open up the final barrier – quality – appropriate funding, planning, hard work by e-learning practitioners, ongoing materials development and continuing staff training are vital in developing effective quality assurance of all aspects of e-learning.

KEY BARRIER MATRIX FOR THE IMPLEMENTATION OF AN E-UNIVERSITY

Table 6.1 summarises key barriers discovered locally in setting up the e-University project. Not a definitive list of all possible barriers, this is a local reflection of problems and solutions encountered at the University of Greenwich.

CONCLUSION

In this chapter we have drawn upon the experiences of one institution in developing an e-University, to highlight key barriers to progress. Not all barriers have been identified, and in this short chapter we cannot reflect in full detail the factors that facilitated our progress. It will not be until this development project is completed and the e-University fully implemented that we will be able to reflect on our experiences and evaluate the outcomes. But to share with a wider audience this identification and unlocking of key barriers is to open up the path to e-learning, with the specific goal of learner achievement in mind.

REFERENCES

Block, P., Perman-Kerr, L. and Katchoff, B. (2001) *E-University of Greenwich Business Modelling Day*. Unpublished Workshop Report by PriceWaterhouse-Coopers, London.

CVCP (2000) *The Business of Borderless Education: UK Perspectives: Analysis and Recommendations* (The Committee of Vice-Chancellors and Principals of the Universities of the UK). London: CVCP.

Faigley, L. (1998) 'Literacy after the revolution: 1996 CCCC Chair's Address', in Taylor, T. and Ward, I. (eds) *Literacy Theory in the Age of the Internet* (pp. 3–16). New York: Columbia University Press.

Hall, B. (2001) *E-Learning Guidebook*. Available at http://brandon-hall.com (accessed March 2004).

Humphreys, J. (1998) *Framework for Learning*. Unpublished Learning and Teaching Committee Report, University of Greenwich, London.

Jameson, J. and Squires, D. (2000) 'Teaching new media composition studies in a lifelong learning context'. Alt-J, *Association for Learning Technology Journal*, 8(3).

Jordan, G. and Ryan, M. (1999) 'Designing a distance curriculum to harness the potential of asynchronous computer conferencing: an example from a Masters programme in continuing professional development', in Collis, B. and Oliver, R. (eds) *Proceedings of Ed-Media 1999 World Conference*. Seattle, Washington, 19–24 June 1999.

Table 6.1 Key barriers to the development of an e-University

Key barrier	Nature of the problem	How to unlock the barrier
Institutional distractions	• Institutional distractions and lack of focus • Confusion about e-learning institutional vision	• Agree terms of focus clearly with senior managers, disseminated throughout project, ensure other issues do not distract staff and keep your eye on the ball • Conceptualise e-University within overall vision for learning; rethink learning re electronic delivery, challenging existing perceptions and prejudices • Brainstorm benefits and opportunities • Draw on ideas and knowledge of enthusiasts • Focus on small-scale effective results; hold regular meetings timetabled with project staff, disseminate vision
Perceptions of leadership	• Perceived unclear leadership • Confused perceptions about decision-making • Feelings of not being informed • Perceptions of top-down structures	• Clear leader(s) identified at a number of levels • Roles and reporting mechanisms and decision-making (e.g. on finances) clarified and disseminated • Disseminate information widely with messages from the observable leader, with feedback loop • Some leadership tasks devolved to sub-projects to maintain progress
Skills	• Lack of skills of staff involved • Staff with appropriate existing skills not identified • Models of learning selected inappropriate for e-learning • New, unproven VLE introduced; long-used, proven VLE sidelined	• Staff development • Identify and involve e-learning champions • Identification of appropriate pedagogical models for implementation; staff development, mentoring and guidance in models of learning • Identification of all requirements for VLE, mapped against facilities from a range of platforms; maintain an 'e-toolkit' of different platforms while evaluating all

Key barrier	Nature of the problem	How to unlock the barrier
e-critics and communication problems	• e-University project perceived as a threat by some e-critics or not considered at all by many	• Dissemination of information about project through individual discussions at school and subgroup level • Use internal publicity mechanisms (e.g. newsletters) to market project • Consider views of e-critics, engage staff, acknowledge problems, provide answers
Staffing	• Staff involved already overloaded	• Delegation of tasks where possible • Cascading of specialist skills
Quality	• Risk to staff re poor e-learning practice and no funds for QA • Risk to staff/institution reputation • Risk to staff re poor e-materials, lack of support and training	• Attention to all aspects of QA – funding identified, planning and delivery monitored • No shortcuts in quality assurance processes and checks on e-delivery; staff development in these • Ongoing materials development and staff training re quality

Laurillard, D. (1993) *Rethinking University Teaching: A Framework for the Effective Use of Educational Technology*. London: Routledge.

Moll, L.C. and Whitmore, K.F. (1993) 'Classroom practice: moving from individual transmission to social transaction', in Foreman, E.A., Minick, N. and Addison Stone, C. (eds) *Contexts for Learning – Sociocultural Dynamics in Children's Development*. Oxford: Oxford University Press.

Quality Assurance Agency for Higher Education (QAA) (1999) *Guidelines on the Quality Assurance of Distance Learning*. Cheltenham: QAA. Available at http://www.qaa.ac.uk/public/dlg/contents.htm (accessed March 2004).

Schön, D. (1983) *The Reflective Practitioner: How Professionals Think in Action*. London: Temple Smith.

University of Greenwich (2000) *e-University Project Booklet*. Unpublished Steering Group Report, London: University of Greenwich.

Werner, T. (2001) *To Successfully Implement E-Learning, Forget What You Know About Change*. QualTeam, Inc. Available at http://brandon-hall.com (accessed March 2004).

Yin, R.K. (1994) *Case Study Research: Design and Methods* (2nd edn) (ASRM Series, vol. 5). London: Sage.

7

Ensuring quality in computer-based assessment

Christine Steven and Stan Zakrzewski

INTRODUCTION

What exactly is quality? It would be so much simpler if quality were an easily defined and unambiguous concept. Quality is a many-faceted attribute and there are a multitude of both formal and informal definitions to be found. Within the context of software, quality has been described as 'hard to define, impossible to measure and easy to recognise' (Kitchenham, 1990). Quality is not absolute since it means different things in different situations and to different people. It is multi-dimensional in that many factors contribute to its being acceptable or not – the easily measured aspects of quality are not always the most important. Quality is also subject to constraints and is frequently about accepting compromises. Cost is an obvious constraint, not only within the financial aspects but also with regard to people, hardware availability and time. Many people have defined their own quality criteria; McCall (1977), Boehm (1978) and Watts (1987) have all admitted that the criteria themselves are not independent, but that they interact with each other causing conflict. Although the work undertaken by these people was originally in the area of software production it may be argued that there are many similarities when producing computer-based assessments and that the solution to providing the best-quality computer-based assessment (CBA) systems is one that produces an optimum balance of criteria rather than an ideal solution.

In a CBA system there are many stakeholders who will judge the quality of the final product. The main criteria they will use to assess quality will depend upon their personal involvement. The CBA system stakeholders include management, academic, support and administrative staff together with external examiners or verifiers, other experts in the field and students who will be sitting the examinations. They will assess the quality of the CBA system through a pedagogic, operational, technical or financial perspective depending upon their roles and responsibilities in the system.

PEDAGOGIC ISSUES

Students who take the CBA examinations will want to feel that the tests themselves have been integrated into their curriculum and that the examinations are error-free. Students who are new to this system of assessment will be more convinced of the quality of the approach if they have had training in how to use the software and pre-exposure to the different question types they may encounter in the examination. Academic staff who can show they are committed to this type of assessment will further enhance the views of students of the quality of the system, and the reliability of the process and results obtained. Academic staff will view the quality of a system such as this from the perspective of the ease of producing questions that are acceptable to relevant professional bodies and external examiners. Professional bodies and external examiners in turn will expect questions to be well designed, testing the whole of the curriculum in a sensible and acceptable manner.

OPERATIONAL ISSUES

Academic staff and support staff need to feel confidant that all issues concerning CBA implementation have been raised (Zakrzewski and Bull, 1998), and that procedures have been put in place to deal with any eventuality. When users of the system can see that they have a full and detailed written set of procedures to follow, their confidence in the quality of the proposed system is increased.

TECHNICAL ISSUES

All those involved with a CBA system, whether from the point of view of taking the assessment or being responsible for the delivery of the tests, are conscious that there is a high probability of technical problems arising. This is inevitable when dealing with computer-based systems. There is the possibility that computers break down, or answer files are lost. When the list of possible risks has been considered (Zakrzewski and Steven, 2000) and solutions put in place should these risks manifest themselves, then all concerned can be more confident that the final product will be of good quality.

FINANCIAL ISSUES

Finally, but perhaps most importantly, there is the issue of finances to be considered. All stakeholders need to be made aware that there is support, both monetary and moral, from senior management. If it can be shown that the running of CBA assessments is cost-effective (Zakrzewski and Bull, 1998), in terms of both time and effort expended by staff and students alike, then managers are more likely to support the continuing development of these systems.

QUALITY VIEWED THROUGH A CBA MODEL

The quality of the system depends upon a structured approach to its design and implementation where pedagogic, operational, technical and financial issues are mapped to their corresponding risks. A generic model for the implementation of computer-based assessment (CBA) systems (Zakrzewski and Steven, 2000) describes five segments: Planning, Risk analysis and management, Assessment design, Evolutionary development, and Evaluation. These segments constitute what is termed the 'Catherine Wheel'.

QUALITY AS VIEWED BY THE STAKEHOLDERS

Quality stakeholders view quality not through a structured approach to CBA implementation, but through:

- *Integration* with current university assessment systems.
- *Staffing issues*, particularly staff development in objective test design.
- *Examination design* and the appropriateness of the objective test questions at higher education levels 1,2,3 to the knowledge and skills being assessed.
- Endorsement by external examiners and advisers of *examination designs*.
- The thoroughness of the *system testing* procedures before the examination period.
- *System integrity* in terms of student conduct, invigilation, security and back-up procedures.

- *Student issues* and in particular student anxiety about a new assessment method.
- *Annual review* of procedures, student performance and costs resulting in a quality assurance report.

MAPPING THE VIEWS OF STAKEHOLDERS TO CBA MODEL SEGMENTS

Risk analysis and management identifies risks and proposes strategies to eliminate them or at least reduce their likelihood of occurring. Risks in turn identify quality assurance issues which are mapped to segments of the systems model (Zakrzewski and Steven, 2000) as shown in Table 7.1.

Table 7.1 Stakeholder views

Segment	Stakeholder view
Planning	Integration
Assessment design	Staffing issues (academic) Examination design
Evolutionary development	Student issues Staffing issues (technical) System integrity System testing
Evaluation	Review

Integration

Planning concerns integration. The framework under which the CBA system will operate must be established. Personnel and their roles and responsibilities must be identified. The CBA system cannot stand alone and therefore must be integrated with the existing institutional assessment procedures and existing documentation.

Staffing issues (academic)

Staff development in effective question design and how CBA systems operate at universities are paramount quality assurance issues. They will form an integral part of the annual staff development programme of the university and should be entered in the staff development events directory.

Academic staff should debate the purpose of testing, what abilities and knowledge can be tested in this way and the suitability of objective testing for the purpose intended. They should discuss the advantages and disadvantages of using objective tests and the importance of test balance in identifying and examining both low and higher order cognitive skills. Academic staff must be introduced to a wide variety of question types (Bull and McKenna, 2001) and be given examples on how they may be used in testing differing skills levels (CAA Centre, 2001). They need to be instructed in effective question design and then to practise objective test construction.

In the second stage of the staff development session, the operation of the assessment system at the university will be described. Academic staff will want to see the arena where the examinations will take place and will require documentation outlining system policies and procedures. Roles and responsibilities of management, external moderators, external advisers, support and academic staff must be outlined. Contingency arrangements in the event of a station crash or system failure must be described. Academic staff will be shown the functions and capabilities of the software including its reporting function and, wherever possible, new staff should be encouraged to see the system in operation before their examination is run.

Examination design

Examination specifications show 'test balance'. The construction of the examination specification has evolved from a model (Heard *et al.*, 1997) based on Bloom's taxonomy of educational objectives. It enables the designer to subdivide the examination into topics and relates each topic to a level of learning. Topics reflect learning outcomes of the module. The total number of questions in each topic and the total number of questions for each level of learning indicate 'test balance'. The purpose of the examination specification is to enable academics to reflect on the 'balance' of the examination before design begins.

Academic staff use specifications to design their examinations. Objective test questions should be realistic, up-to-date and unambiguous. They should not be trivial or obscure but should test the relevant skill ability, grouped in a logical sequence according to knowledge, or skills being tested (CAA Centre, 2001).

Student issues

Those students who are likely to be taking CBA examinations, normally those in groups exceeding 100, should be canvassed very early in their university life so that their experiences and expectations of CBA may be identified. Any students who express a major aversion to using a computer should be given a paper-based examination containing identical material in an attempt to alleviate undue anxiety. A series of short (ten questions) computer-based tests (CBTs) should be provided for students throughout their first semester so that they can become familiar with both the software navigation system and the type of question likely to be asked. Comments should be requested from the students so that the questions and the method of introduction can be amended if required. As a result of such actions, initial CBTs taken at the University of Luton, named 'tasters', were amended to give feedback associated with each question response and a detailed set of instructions on the examination procedures was provided as an *aide-mémoire* (Steven and Hesketh, 1999).

Staffing issues (technical)

Technical training is an investment in the system and should not be viewed merely as a cost by managers. CBA is a team effort involving students, academic staff and support staff. The support staff play a crucial role in ensuring that the system performs reliably and as expected by the users (students). Support staff will be required to understand not only the functionality of the software but also how the software presents the questions to the students, records the marks for each question and enables navigation from one question to another. They must be able to install the software, integrate it with current management information systems (e.g. student record system), upgrade the system when required, perform formal system tests at appropriate times and collate results from many servers and/or sites. Such detailed knowledge requires training provided by the software vendor in addition to that provided 'in-house'.

System integrity

System integrity should cover areas such as cheating, invigilation, security and back-up. The first two areas are common to all types of examination but in a CBA system they bring their own problems too. All students will in general be taking the same examination, as space will not be available for a variety of examinations to take place at the same time. IT arenas are not designed with examinations in mind, and the proximity of work-stations is a temptation to view neighbours' screens. There are different techniques that can be used to try to minimise the possibility of students copying answers from each other when using a CBA system. Some systems have the facility to display questions in a random order while others display possible answers in a different sequence, thus making it less likely that adjacent examinees could benefit from looking at their neighbour's monitor. Another possibility is to invest in privacy screens placed on workstation monitors which only enable face-to-face viewing and cut out any attempts to view a workstation from one adjacent to it.

Staff, both academic and technical, need to be on hand for invigilation purposes. The academic staff must be vigilant in their monitoring of students prior to, during and immediately after the examinations. It is vital that the students present identification, and that usernames and passwords can be checked for authenticity (Whittington, 1999).

CBA systems must be secure and have appropriate back-up procedures in place in the event of a workstation or system failure. The examination must be isolated from any system resources that may provide valuable information in answering the questions. This is especially crucial for web-based assessment systems that potentially can link to information sites across the Internet. Security managers (software that isolates examinations from information sources) are generally available from CBA vendors. A system of passwords and student-group identifiers must be used to restrict access to individual examinations. All examinations should be mounted on a dedicated server at the appropriate time and then deleted from the server as soon as the examination is completed. Passwords and student-group identifiers will need to be changed periodically. The results must be secure, with access privileges available only to those members of staff responsible for collating the results. The results should be backed up with copies of the results held electronically but off-line (on a floppy disk, zip disk or CD-ROM).

Back-up procedures should be in place in the event of either an individual workstation breakdown or a server collapse. If a workstation collapses during the examination the student should be moved to an 'overflow area' where he or she can resume the examination on a different workstation. If the software does not allow students to resume where they had left off but only allows a restart from the beginning, then a decision must be made as to whether or not there is enough time to restart the examination. If there is not enough time for a restart, students should be given the opportunity to either keep the original results (which may be the case if they were reviewing their answers and the examination had a few minutes left to run) or retake the examination using a hard copy. If the server collapses during the examination, procedures should be in place to activate a back-up server or reschedule the event if there is not time to resume or restart the examination.

System testing

A pre-test of the examination will be required. The aim of the pre-test is to ascertain the reliability and validity of the examination. Pre-tests should be carried out by the academic member of staff responsible for designing the examination and a member of the support services. The pre-test will clarify the suitability of the examination at the level intended, the technical integrity of the examination, the relevance of blind guessing and that 100 per cent can be obtained. A pre-test event log should be maintained which will record the results of the pre-test and any actions that need to be taken. All CBA examinations should be pre-tested before they are sent externally for moderation.

A formal system test is required prior to the examination event. The aim of the formal system test is to ascertain the reliability of the system. The examinations undergo a 'dry run' in the arena that will be used by the students. For web-based systems, the system requires testing on all platforms and browsers to ensure comparability of performance and comparability of presentation. Every question is answered and the results checked to ascertain that they have been accurately stored and are a true reflection of performance at the workstation.

REVIEW

A review board should be set up that would be responsible for the compilation of an annual monitoring report. This should coincide with the institution's annual monitoring cycle. The report should address all issues outlined above concerning the quality of computer-based assessments. The annual report should be sent to the academic standards committee of the institution and include the following:

- a comparative evaluation of CBA achievement against traditional assessment formats;
- a review of the effectiveness of the staff development programme;
- the effectiveness of risk reduction and elimination procedures;
- staff and student comments and suggestions;
- external examiners' and advisers' comments;
- a detailed cost-benefit analysis;
- recommendations for improvements.

CONCLUSION

No system can please all stakeholders all of the time; but if a good compromise can be reached and it shows that the system being used is producing reliable results within the required timescale, then it may be said to be of good quality. It is vital that the system generates detailed procedures that are based on risk reduction or elimination so that a quality system will be delivered when implemented. The authors maintain that quality is inherent in the generic CBA model, 'The Catherine Wheel', as identified by Zakrzewski and Steven (2000).

REFERENCES

Boehm, B. (1978) *Characteristics of Software Quality*. New York: North-Holland.

Bull, J. and McKenna, C. (2001) *Blueprint for Computer-assisted Assessment*. CAA Centre, University of Luton.

Computer Assisted Assessment (CAA) Centre (2001) *Final Report*. Available at http://caacentre.lboro.ac.uk (accessed February 2004).

Heard, S., Nicol, J. and Heath, S. (1997) *Setting Effective Objective Tests*. MERTal Publications, University of Aberdeen.

Kitchenham, B. (1990) 'Software metrics', in Rook, P. (ed.) *Software Reliability Handbook*. Amsterdam: Elsevier Applied Science.

McCall, J. (1977) 'Concepts and definitions of software quality', *Factors in Software Quality*, NTIS, Vol. 1.

Steven, C. and Hesketh, I. (1999) 'Increasing learner responsibility and support with the aid of adaptive and formative assessment using QM design software', in Brown, S., Race, P. and Bull, J. (eds) *Computer-assisted Assessment in Higher Education*. London: Kogan Page.

Watts, R. (1987) *Measuring Software Quality*. Manchester: NCC Publications.

Whittington, D. (1999) 'Technical and security issues', in Brown, S., Race, P. and Bull, J. (eds) *Computer-assisted Assessments in Higher Education*. London: Kogan Page.

Zakrzewski, S. and Bull, J. (1998) 'The mass implementation and evaluation of computer-based assessments', *Assessment and Evaluation in Higher Education*, 23(2), pp. 141–52.

Zakrzewski, S. and Steven, C. (2000) 'A model for computer-based assessment: the Catherine wheel principle', *Assessment and Evaluation in Higher Education*, 25(2), pp. 201–15.

8

ICT and quality in the research process

Adrian Bromage

INTRODUCTION

The development of modern information and communication technologies (ICT) since the early 1980s has been rapid. Personal computers offer previously unimaginable computing power and data-storage capacity. This has occurred alongside the development of powerful and (relatively) user-friendly software tools, and freely available, graphical Internet browsers. The latter have enabled both individuals and organisations to populate 'cyberspace' with sites offering specialised information, software tools and virtual meeting places.

This chapter seeks to examine ways in which such developments can influence the quality of research. Thus it seeks to build upon the work of Blackmore *et al.* (2002) who explored ways in which ICT could ensure quality in the teaching of research methods. Blackmore *et al.* identify five generic research capabilities: being innovative, working independently, setting, and solving, problems, and analysing critically. They then identify three broad generic research prerequisites for these capacities: a body of disciplinary knowledge, techniques used within the discipline, and higher order cognitive skills, concentrating on how ICT might contribute to teaching and learning that develops the latter. I seek to concentrate upon the research process, and will focus on the extent to which ICT tools and resources might affect quality in relation to the two research prerequisites that Blackmore *et al.* did not examine: a body of disciplinary knowledge, and techniques used within the discipline.

The approach taken is to explore how ICT might impact both positively and negatively on these prerequisites across four phases of the research process: reviewing existing knowledge, designing the research, data collection, and data analysis. Rather than attempting a comprehensive description and review of the available ICT resources, the level of description will be broad and generic, sprinkled with representative examples. This analysis is timely; Fazackerley (2003) reports on a proposed new code of practice for research that is being drafted by the Department for the Environment, Food and Rural Affairs (DEFRA), the Biotechnology and Biological Sciences Research Council (BBSRC) and the Natural Environment Research Council (NERC). The code emphasises the quality of the research process, with the aim of ensuring that research yields results that are rigorous, replicable and appropriate. It is notable that many academic disciplines have set out their own 'internal' measures that researchers take to similar ends.

To the extent that research and teaching are synergistic, those same issues must impact on the quality of teaching activities. A great deal of higher education comprises research-related education, for example, Ph.D. and M.Phil. by research, and undergraduate programmes in disciplines as diverse as psychology and physics. Hattie and Marsh's (1996) meta-analysis of the literature concerning the beneficial relationship between research and teaching identifies two broad views. They are a 'conventional wisdom' position, and a more well-developed view that the abilities which underlie good teaching and good research are the same. Hattie and Marsh trace the historical roots of the latter to Humboldt's notion that researcher and student are unified in the common pursuit of knowledge, suggestive of an apprenticeship in the craft of research as a means to know the world under the mentorship of those skilled in that craft. It is arguable that implicit within this is a notion of 'Socratic dialogue', and it is perhaps this that Brew and Boud (1995) tap into with their notion that teaching can be a learning process for both the student and teacher, and that this is the juncture of research and teaching.

Coate *et al.* (2001, p. 159) note that there is little empirical evidence presented in this body of literature, and they conduct an empirical investigation into the extent to which research and teaching are connected in the everyday lives of academics. They found disciplinary differences in perceptions of the integration of teaching and research, and attribute this to differing ontological standpoints. Those whose disciplines have an underlying constructivist ontology, such as history or some approaches to sociology, may be more likely to perceive synergies than those whose disciplines have an underlying realist ontology, such as physics or chemistry.

The authors found that the academics in their study held the positive influence of research on teaching to be that students perceive research-active academics to have more 'authority' to teach a subject, their enthusiasm 'rubs off' on to their students, they incorporate relevant and up-to-date material in their teaching, and they teach from firsthand experience. Then again, disciplinary differences were found. Academics' research interests tend to directly influence their teaching throughout undergraduate work in the humanities, whereas in the sciences the influence is stronger on final-year undergraduate and postgraduate-level teaching. Positively, teaching obliges academic researchers to articulate their ideas and expose them to challenges from students. The students' own ideas can stimulate new research directions, as can engaging in the teaching of unfamiliar areas. Research-based teaching can lead to a situation where research students' work accounts for a significant amount of a department's research activities.

Coate *et al.* examine independent relationships between research and teaching. They conclude that they are difficult to separate clearly, and there exist scholarly activities that can inform both teaching and research activities. Coate *et al.* do, however, suggest that in some cases highly specialised research is conducted by non-teaching staff, and so is necessarily separate from teaching, and they identify a more general tendency for staff in a department to differentiate between those who are research-active and those who are not. Coate *et al.*'s exploration of negative relationships between research and teaching indicates that they tend to be related to academics' personal dispositions, such as levels of interest in working with students or the constraints of available time, energy and commitment, the latter falling under what Hattie and Marsh (1996) call a 'scarcity model'. Other negative relationships tend to be associated with structural constraints such as spatially separate locations for teaching and research, financial considerations, and paperwork demands from, for example (and with some irony), the Quality Assurance Agency.

Coate *et al.* conclude that the realities of university life are that research and teaching exist in a variety of relationships, and they distinguish between research, teaching and scholarship, arguing that while good teaching can take place independently of research, neither can take place without scholarship. Their distinction will be adopted within this chapter, to highlight any overlap between research and scholarly activity so as to identify the extent to which ICT tools and resources can enhance the quality of both activities. One question that will be addressed is the extent to which ICT resources have changed the nature of the whole enterprise of research: Are there 'magic button' technologies that can generate the answers we seek at the press of a button?

REVIEWING EXISTING KNOWLEDGE

The first phase of a research project in any discipline is to conduct a review of relevant literature, to establish both 'the state of the art' and a research direction that will build upon the existing literature. This is arguably an act of 'scholarship' in the sense proposed by Coate *et al.* (2001). To this extent, any enhancements of the quality of this phase of a research project that may be attributed to ICT resources will arguably apply also to academics' teaching activities, whether research-based or not.

Communication and information technologies (ICT) have for some years now played an increasing role in the contemporary university library. The original stimulus was the 'Follett Report' of 1993, and subsequently the 'Dearing Report' of 1997, which reinforced the drive to develop the ICT capabilities within academic libraries. Most academic libraries in the UK now have an online catalogue, links to various external databases and electronic journals through the Joint Academic Network (JANET) and the World Wide Web, and access to specialist CD-ROM databases. The effect of such resources has been substantial: it has greatly speeded up the process of finding particular texts when compared to using card catalogues. The online catalogues also facilitate browsing of books and journals that cover similar topics, through the use of selective searches.

Access to the World Wide Web brings the information-seeker to academic publications worldwide; thus it is far easier for academics to keep abreast of the latest developments within their discipline. There have been instances where publishers have used the World Wide Web to rapidly release important research papers into the public domain. For example, on 14 March 2003, *The New England Journal of Medicine* used their 'table of contents service', emailed to subscribers to the service, to publicise the early release on their website of an article concerning an HIV-1 Fusion Inhibitor in advance of the 29 May issue of their journal. This was in response to its gaining approval by the FDA on 13 March. The online edition of the *British Medical Journal* incorporates hyperlinks between articles and subsequent articles in which they are cited, including those in other journals. This facility helps browsing of related works, which in turn ensures that nothing is missed. One potential drawback is that this could lead to a 'tunnel vision' that inhibits academics from gaining insights into works that are not directly related to their particular interests, a point that will be developed below.

There also exist 'information gateways' of discipline-related materials. For example, the 'Social Science Information Gateway' features links to a wide range of websites that relate to various strands of the social sciences. The 'Engineering' strand of the 'Internet Guide to Engineering, Mathematics and Computing' provides access to a mere 150 online journals. However, the available resources differ across academic disciplines: www.freemedicaljournals.com makes 980 full-text online medical journals available. Despite these inequalities, such resources are, along with electronic catalogues, of value to those who for whatever reason spend the bulk of their time off-campus (e.g. those engaged in field research, or part-time researchers).

Another valuable resource is the academic newsgroup. Newsgroups enable academics to share and test ideas, opinions and so on with peers, and to solicit advice. In the UK, the Joint Information Services Committee (JISC) sponsors 'JISCmail', a mailing list service for the UK Further and Higher Education communities that hosts seventy-seven newsgroups which represent the majority of academic disciplines. Online academic conferences offer a more formal forum. Such services can be a boon for those who for whatever reason find themselves without a local peer group, and offer all academics more immediate contact with a global community of peers than would otherwise be possible.

It has been argued that ICT can thus act to level out resource inequalities between institutions. There are a few cracks in this rosy picture. As soon as one strays from refereed journals and academic sites, the quality of websites is, to say the least, highly variable. Outside of the 'academic safety net', one's critical skills are all one has to discern the 'crock of gold' from the 'crock of rubbish'. Another issue concerns social cohesiveness. There are a finite number of hours in a day, so increasing contacts with colleagues across the world who share one's professional interests probably means decreasing contacts with one's departmental colleagues. This may lead to more individualised research projects perhaps with increased collaboration with colleagues beyond one's immediate physical vicinity, and so act to reduce the local collaboration of colleagues on research projects.

This is perhaps symptomatic of a mode of communication that Lievrouw (1998) argues has emerged from a belief in the positive power of communications technologies and a cultural attitude of self-interest, which she terms 'heterotopic communication', and summarises thus:

> we acquire and use information competitively, treating communication as a commodity exchange; we adopt an outward perspective of globalism while practising a kind of electronic separatism, creating many small and specialized channels for interaction with others who share our particular beliefs.

In terms of the quality of the research that is produced by particular individuals, this is likely to be enhanced by their ability to interact with a global community of scholars who share the same interests; however, the possibilities for academic 'stars' to positively influence the quality of their immediate colleagues' research may be reduced. These scenarios might be counteracted by the development of a collegiate culture within the local setting.

There is one final consideration. The quality of a research project arguably rests heavily on the research question at its heart, which must be such that it addresses the chosen research issue. Indeed, Sir Harry Kroto (2002), 1996 winner of the Nobel Prize for Chemistry, comments in a recent article in *The Times Higher Education Supplement*, 'after a while, I made an empirical discovery. I stumbled upon the fascinating rule: the act of framing a question precisely was key to understanding.' Kroto cites a saying of the ancient Chinese philosopher Confucius, 'I seek not the answer – but to understand the question', and he comments, 'Dammit, Confucius got there first – but at least I know more quantum physics than he did.' The latter perhaps illustrates the message of this section; while the framing of a research question arguably remains an issue of skilled judgement and insightful thinking, ICT can ensure that the researcher has access to a wide body of up-to-date knowledge that can inform such judgements on demand.

RESEARCH DESIGN

This phase of the research process, matching the research design to the research problem, might initially appear not to entail scholarship in the sense proposed by Coate *et al.* (2001). However, in order to critically evaluate published research one needs among other things to understand the research methods used. To this extent it may be said that while a divergence exists between scholarship and research activity, engaging in either requires one to have a firm grounding in research methods.

There exist several electronic resources for research designers. There are a large number of academic websites describing research design and methods for different academic disciplines. There also exist what are in effect expert systems for research design. Peer Review Emulator is a CD-ROM designed to assist those who are preparing social science research proposals. The latter can interface with Methodologists' Toolchest, a CD-ROM offering guidance to research designers on, for example, appropriate research models for particular research questions. Such resources can help to ensure quality in the research process insofar as there is less scope for researchers to make a fundamental error in their choices, or to overlook some important aspect of research design.

However, even if the research method and design are appropriate, the quality of a research project rests heavily on the related decisions concerning the nature of the raw data to be collected. They must be such that they are appropriate to the research problem that is to be addressed. Such decisions require researchers to exercise their higher order cognitive skills.

THE PROCESS OF DATA COLLECTION

Academics have exploited computers in their research procedures for the past fifty years. The dawn of the personal computing age in the late 1970s has led to this becoming common practice across many disciplines. Some researchers now have fingertip access to primary data sources. For example, historians can purchase CD-ROM archives, such as 'Domesday Explorer' which features a complete translation of the *Domesday Book*, along with images of the entire original manuscript. Other academics (e.g. economists and health researchers) can access a range of websites that feature collections of relevant raw data. Indeed, historians can access the UK government site which features datasets from the very first to the latest population census.

Other academics must still collect their own data, and they can exploit ICT in different ways. Engineers might control research procedures using computers, while experimental psychologists commonly run their entire procedure on computer. This particular 'magic button' facility has a direct influence on the quality of a research project, as it can help to ensure consistency across trials. There is unfortunately a fly in the ointment. Some procedures, particularly those of the experimental psychologist, depend upon accurate timing to the last millisecond. While a personal computer can be set up to do this, its internal architecture is such that it cannot deliver the level of accuracy that it appears to promise (Hammond *et al.*, 2000). This is fine, so long as one is aware that in some cases purpose-built timers must be used. It remains however a relatively obscure technical issue of which it is probably fair to say the majority of computer users are unaware.

One interesting feature of ICT is that the facilities it offers make it possible for a researcher to collect huge volumes of raw data with comparatively little effort. Data of a qualitative nature may be collected using electronic surveys with relative ease as compared to traditional paper-based surveys. For example, an HTML page may be set up as a 'front end' that will automatically store participants' responses in a database, and the page's URL circulated to potential participants by email or by posting it on an Internet newsgroup. Quantitative data may be collected automatically and comparatively cheaply through 'datalogging'. Here large numbers of data-gathering devices are linked directly to a central database and the information is recorded automatically. Engineers may use dataloggers to collect data, for example, on the dynamic performance of a car or a bridge. Their use is not restricted to engineering. VLEs such as WebCT have what could be regarded as built-in datalogging capabilities, insofar as the software automatically counts the number of times each student has used particular facilities.

The ICT capabilities identified above conform to my definition of the 'magic button'. It is true to say that they have made some research projects that were in the past impractical a realistic possibility, and made it possible to explore the new research frontier of cyberspace. It is arguable that this does not necessarily mean that the quality of such research is high, since, regardless of the media, this depends upon its design and execution. Such capabilities can however help researchers to refine the quality of the knowledge base of a discipline. ICT has the potential to facilitate the exploration of new research by making it possible to collect data that would previously have been 'out of reach'.

DATA ANALYSIS

A similar general point to be made in relation to the design phase also applies to this phase of the research process. Again, while a divergence exists between being actively engaged in the research process and scholarship, in order to critically evaluate published research one needs a firm grounding in data-analysis techniques. Regardless of the particular techniques deployed to gather raw data, the process of analysis tends to follow the same broad pattern across disciplines: organising the data in order to bring out any patterns within it. This holds for both qualitative and quantitative data, although the way it is achieved differs markedly with each type of data. For these reasons this section is organised so as to differentiate between the two types of data.

It was noted in the previous section that recent developments in ICT have facilitated the collection of large corpuses of raw data. This raises several issues for the data-analysis phase of a research project, regardless of whether the raw data are quantitative or qualitative. Beginning with quantitative data, software packages exist that are designed to ease the load for those who work with large datasets. It is well known that spread-sheet software such as Excel, Access and SPSS makes it possible for individuals to conduct numerical analyses of large volumes of numerical data using complex mathematical techniques that would be difficult and time consuming to implement by hand. However, the usefulness of these tools has its limits. Where quantitative data have been collected using a datalogger, the resulting raw dataset can be so vast that it would take many years to simply read through it once. Inferential statistical tests, such as the Students' 't' test, tend to be designed to be accurate with datasets up to a finite size, measured in hundreds of items rather than thousands, a relatively obscure technical point of which some academics may not necessarily be aware.

Software tools also exist that support the processes of qualitative data analysis. Such tools enable changes to be made to the evolving system of text segments, codes and theoretical notes which are laborious when working on hard copies of, say, interview transcripts with paper, pencil and scissors. They also act as an electronic filing system where materials are accessible at the 'touch of a button'. While this does not itself fit my definition of a 'magic button', the flexibility it affords can arguably raise the quality of the interpretative analysis, insofar as it facilitates the process of data analysis. Perhaps the most well-known commercial examples of such software are Nvivo, and ATLAS/ti, which is promoted as being a 'knowledge workbench'. More will be said about such tools below. A free software package along similar lines is AnSWR (http://www.cdc.gov/hiv/software/answr.htm).

The next set of techniques to be examined are closer to the 'magic button' definition. Automated data mining, algorithmic techniques for identifying patterns that are deployed in Knowledge Discovery in Databases (KDD) (Fayyad *et al.*, 1996), may be applied to quantitative datasets that are too vast for a researcher to explore 'by eye' in order to generate models of any patterns that exist within the raw data. Fayyad *et al.* illustrate the application of KDD in diverse subject areas, from astronomy to marketing. Many commercially available data-mining software packages are based around statistical tools such as correspondence analysis, cluster analysis and multidimensional scaling. Analogously, there exist software packages for qualitative data analysis that incorporate techniques such as automated content analysis, and may be applied to very large datasets of textual qualitative data to generate descriptive results regarding, for example, how texts cluster together in terms of their content or the way that content has been expressed. Qualrus is a software package that uses intelligent computational strategies (e.g. case-based reasoning, machine learning and semantic networks) to generate such insights. Wordstat, an add-in module for the database software 'Simstat', can perform automatic content analysis on a document or selected sections of a document, and can cluster documents in terms of similarity of their content, as well as performing several other useful operations. Perhaps the most intriguing is CodeRead, an MS-DOS program which 'learns' approximations of the way a particular researcher breaks a text into smaller quotations and assigns them to conceptual categories from examples of previously coded texts, and then applies them to new texts (Perrin, 2000). Arguably such programs form a distinct genre that might be defined as 'mini-me' rather than 'magic button' software.

To this extent ICT can extend the 'grasp' of researchers well beyond their 'reach', as it were. The kinds of descriptive analyses supported may be considered as low-level interpretative activities, insofar as they summarise patterns in the raw data. With quantitative data this might yield, for example, clusters of related faults in an airliner. However, this descriptive analysis is only part of the overall picture. Gordon (1978), writing on cluster analysis, explains that two different subject experts with the same level of expertise who interpret the same dendrogram or tree diagram can reach different conclusions as to the boundaries of plausible clusters. Furthermore, different clustering algorithms applied to the same raw data are likely to yield dendrograms that look quite different, and there is no consensus among the experts on which algorithm is 'best'. With qualitative data, the yield might be clusters of related quotes or segments of a larger text, or individuals whose narratives demonstrate a similar weighting of certain identified clusters of text segments. The same general point also applies here.

Whether quantitative or qualitative, the machine-generated descriptions of both quantitative and qualitative data that have been validated by the researcher must themselves be subjected to further interpretation in order to generate higher level and more abstract interpretative insights (e.g. why a particular pattern is found in the data and with what practical implications). This remains a skilled activity that depends upon the researcher's higher order cognitive skills. It is arguably at this level that the quality of the knowledge base of a discipline tends to be refined and developed.

A further issue has been identified. Fielding (1993) comments on the then available software for qualitative data analysis:

> the existing software contains an implicit theory of qualitative analysis, one which is not conducive to the full range of analytic postures customarily found in this eclectic field. Insofar as existing software presumes a generic theory of qualitative analysis, it largely relates to the conventional, but by no means universal, grounded theory approach. Those preferring hermeneutic approaches, ethnomethodology, conversation analysis or holistic analysis are less well-served.

Coffey *et al.* (1996) make a similar point. Indeed, the current version of the software package ATLAS/ti is, like the original, designed to facilitate a particular model of grounded theorising developed by Strauss and Corbin (1990). Their model aroused the ire of Strauss' former collaborator Glaser (1992), who argues that it actually represents full, forced, conceptual description. While the software supports other forms of analysis that rely on the generic processes of segmenting a text into quotations and assigning related quotations into conceptual categories, the danger is that the naive researcher may uncritically assume that the supported model is the 'best' way to approach data analysis, when in fact it may not be the most appropriate to their own research approach, aims or what might be termed their 'heuristic preferences' (Polanyi, 1958), the ontological and epistemological assumptions of the theoretical tradition in which they work.

CONCLUSION

The arguments set out in this chapter raise a number of issues for those who engage in both scholarly activities and research-related activities such as research-based teaching, research projects and the supervision of research. While anyone who participates in any such research-related activities should be aware of the issues and how they relate to their own work, this is arguably of particular importance for those who supervise research projects.

The use of ICT tools and resources in the research process can enable previously out-of-reach questions to be explored, and to this extent they have the potential to enrich the quality of an academic discipline's knowledge-base. It has been argued that 'magic button' software exists to an extent in relation to the processes of data-gathering and analysis. For example, there exists software that automates research procedures, data may be gathered by datalogging, and descriptive data analysis may be achieved using automated data mining for quantitative datasets that are too vast for human comprehension, and to a lesser extent for qualitative data analysis.

However, in terms of the quality of the subsequent research the emerging picture is one of partial gains and potential traps. One of the greatest dangers is that such technologies can beguile the unwary, and this can apply equally to those involved in all the categories of research activities outlined above. The old maxim 'garbage in garbage out' still holds. If the research design or the nature of the data collected are inappropriate to the research question, then the quality of the research project will be poor, regardless of whether ICT tools have been exploited in the research process. It has also been argued that the very architecture of a personal computer can compromise the accuracy of the raw data collected during an automated experimental procedure.

A similar point may be made in relation to data analysis, although here there is an additional issue. Software such as data-mining tools can facilitate the process of analysing both qualitative and quantitative data, insofar as they automate the descriptive level of analysis, so freeing the researcher from time-consuming procedures, often involving complex mathematics. To the extent that the possibility of human error is removed, the software may be said to enhance quality. However, the central issue here relates to the process of moving from a descriptive level of analysis to a more abstract one. The quality of the analysis also depends to a large extent upon the interpretation of the results of such procedures by an expert, as Gordon's (1978) argument in relation to the interpretation of machine-produced clusters illustrates.

In summary, ICT resources can help to enhance the quality of the research process. A tool such as 'Methodologist's Toolchest' can help to ensure that the design and procedure adopted for a research project are appropriate. There also exist software tools that can automate certain aspects and even approximate the researcher's own judgements (Perrin, 2000). Perhaps the danger of such tools, especially those that automate various processes, is that they might beguile a researcher into assuming that the quality of the resulting research will 'automatically' be assured. This applies equally to all of the categories of research activities that have been discussed in this chapter. For the researcher, the trick in all of this is to realise that the available ICT tools have limits, to be aware of what they are, and to remember that the overall quality of a research project depends ultimately upon the application of their own higher order cognitive skills.

REFERENCES

Blackmore, P., Roach, M. and Dempster, J. (2002) 'The use of ICT in education for research and development', in S. Fallows, and R. Bhanot (eds) *Educational Development through Information and Communications Technology*. London: Kogan Page.

Brew, A. and Boud, D. (1995) Teaching and research: establishing the vital link with learning. *Higher Education* 24(1), pp. 261–73.

Coate, K., Barnett, R. and Williams, G. (2001) Relationships between teaching and research in higher education in England. *Higher Education Quarterly* 55(2), pp. 158–74.

Coffey, A., Holbrook, B. and Atkinson, P. (1996) Qualitative data analysis: technologies and representations. *Sociological Research Online* 1(1) [Online journal]. Available at: http://www.socresonline.org.uk/socresonline/1/1/4. html (accessed February 2004).

Dearing, R. (1997) *Higher Education in the Learning Society: Report of the National Committee* (The Dearing Report). Crown Copyright: Great Britain.

Fayyad, U., Piatetsky-Shapiro, G. and Smyth, P. (1996) From data mining to knowledge discovery in databases. *AI Magazine* 17(3), pp. 37–54.

Fazackerley, A. (2003) Research funders up stakes on quality. *The Times Higher Education Supplement*, 14 March, p. 9.

Fielding, N. (1993) Analysing qualitative data by computer. *Social Research Update* 1. Available at http://www.soc.surrey.ac.uk/sru/SRU1.html (accessed February 2004).

Follett, B. (1993) *Joint Funding Council's Libraries Review Group: Report* (The Follett Report). Bristol: HEFC. Available at http://www.niss.ac.uk/education/hefc/follett/report (accessed February 2004).

Glaser, B.G (1992) *Emergence vs Forcing: Basics of Grounded Theory Analysis*. Mill Valley, CA: Sociology Press.

Gordon, A.D. (1978) *Classification*. London: Chapman and Hall.

Hammond, N.V., Beringer, J., Plant, R.R., Quinlan, P. and Schneider, W. (2000) 'Timing issues in experimental control', in *Proceedings of CiP2000: Computers in Psychology*. University of York, 29–31 March.

Hattie, J. and Marsh, H.W. (1996) The relationship between research and teaching: a meta-analysis. *Review of Educational Research* 66(4), pp. 507–42.

Kroto, H. (2002) Harry Kroto. *The Times Higher Education Supplement*, 22 November, p. 15.

Lievrouw, L.A. (1998) Our own devices: heterotopic communication, discourse and culture in the information society. *The Information Society* 14(2) (April–June), pp. 83–96.

Perrin, A.J. (2000) CodeRead: a multiplatform coding engine for text-based data. Paper presented at the American Sociological Association Annual Meeting, Washington, DC, 16 August. Available at: http://www.unc.edu/~aperrin/Code Read/coderead-asa2000.pdf (accessed February 2004).

Polanyi, M. (1958) *Personal Knowledge: Towards a Post-critical Philosophy*. London: Routledge & Kegan Paul.

Strauss, A. and Corbin, J. (1990) *Basics of Qualitative Research: Techniques and Procedures for Developing Grounded Theory*. Thousand Oaks, CA: Sage.

9

ICT: a major step for disabled students

Pamela Eastwood

SUMMARY

This chapter reviews the benefits that can accrue to the disabled student through the use of ICT. It argues from the perspective of someone who has direct experience of this issue over many years of study at three higher education institutions and at all steps from B.Sc. through to Ph.D.

The chapter is written from a UK perspective and makes reference to local legislation, institutions and organisations; however, I hope that the principles outlined are transferable to other countries.

INTRODUCTION

In the UK, students with a disability are only 40 per cent as likely to enter higher education as their able-bodied peers (Curtis 2002), and in the academic year 2000/01 only 4 per cent of all first-year students in higher education had some known form of disability or ill-health (HESA 2003a). Despite these low figures, increased disability awareness, advances in technology, widening of the eligibility criteria for disability allowances, and new legislation have meant that the number of disabled students in the UK has actually been rising. Between 1994/95 and 2000/01, the number of disabled students in their first year in higher education almost doubled, compared to overall intake which was up by around 27 per cent. The greatest increase was in the number of postgraduates. In 2000/01 there were three times as many postgraduates with a known disability as there were in 1994/95 (HESA 2003a, 2003b).

For disabled people, whatever situation in society they find themselves in, the key issue is 'barriers to inclusion' rather than what is actually 'wrong' with the individual, and higher education is no different. Given the opportunity, disabled people are very resourceful and will find ways around problems that would never (have to) occur to a non-disabled person. They know the limitations of their disability better than anyone else. However, they have to be given the opportunity.

From personal experience, the most significant development to break down barriers to higher education for disabled people has been the advances in ICT. Over the past twenty years I have experienced how ICT has made higher education far more accessible to the disabled student. I went from being an undergraduate, who at the beginning of the 1980s was not able to use a university computer at all (no disabled access to the computer centre), to being a home-based Ph.D. student at the beginning of the 2000s with the world at my ICT fingertips. Advances in ICT were literally responsible for my being able to complete my Ph.D. studies.

Computer equipment may be adapted to meet the individual needs and requirements of most disabled students; with specialist software and access to the Internet, this means that there are now options available for disabled students at every stage of their studies. ICT enables the disabled student to:

- transcribe notes/recordings from lectures;
- receive lecture notes/assignments for missed lectures by email, via the Internet or on disc;
- access relevant information sources for assignments or research using library databases and the Internet;
- produce high-quality written work using adapted computer equipment, such as large monitors, adapted keyboards, voice recognition systems;
- submit written work via email or on disc;
- receive lecturer's/supervisor's comments and amended scripts by email or on disc using correction options of word-processing systems such as in MSWord;
- use email to make research contacts, rather than having to post letters or use the telephone;
- use computer technology for presentations.

Most disabilities can now be accommodated, as can periods of absence due to health problems. An added advantage is that most of the above options are available from a base other than the HE establishment, such as home or hospital, thus enabling disabled students to keep up with their studies. Advances in ICT have therefore not only offered a greater number of disabled people the opportunity to enter higher education but, once there, they have also helped them to keep up with their studies.

This chapter starts with a brief examination of the current legislation covering disability and higher education in the UK; it then examines the types of technology and communication software available to help disabled students with their studies.

UK LEGISLATION

Since 2002, with the Special Educational Needs and Disability Act 2001 (SENDA), it has been unlawful for any provider of post-compulsory education to discriminate against disabled students (both current and prospective).

There are two main requirements for higher education institutions. These are that responsible bodies:

1 must not treat a disabled person 'less favourably' than a non-disabled person for reasons related to his or her disability without 'justification'; and
2 will be required by law to make 'reasonable adjustments' to ensure that a disabled student is not placed at a 'substantial disadvantage'.

Some UK students will receive support from sources such as the Disabled Students' Allowance, for adapted computer equipment and specialist software. Here the higher education institution is not expected to cover the same disability support met by another source. However, if not all the needs of the disabled student are met by other sources, the institution may have to provide the additional support.

Most of the Act came into force in 2002, and for universities requirements relating to auxiliary services and aids became law on 1 September 2003. The Act does not define auxiliary aids, but, according to one HE disability coordinator, it is 'taken to include information in alternative formats, web pages, assistive technology, induction loops, provision of support workers to assist with note taking etc.' (Luxford 2003). (Further information on auxiliary aids and examples of discriminatory and non-discriminatory practices may be found in a code of practice which is available from the Disability Rights Commission website: www.drc.org.uk/drc/documents/Post16CoP2.doc.)

The UK also requires each higher education institution to publish disability statements containing information about the facilities for education and research for disabled persons.

The Act has therefore meant that it is now much easier for the disabled student to determine what facilities, assistance and supportive technology are available. A typical university Disability Policy Statement includes information about funding for specialist equipment, specialist support services, and equipment available within the institution and items available on loan. It may outline future activity and development policy, although this is subject to resource constraints and funding uncertainties.

ALTERNATIVE AND ADAPTIVE TECHNOLOGY

Hundreds of products are available which enable the disabled person to communicate effectively using a computer. Technologies range from Microsoft Accessibility Options, which allow the computer screen to be customised (e.g. background display colours, menu/font size), to incredibly complex pieces of equipment. Over the past few years many of these products have become relatively inexpensive and some, such as voice-recognition systems, are now promoted as mainstream consumer products.

Products (hardware and software) may be categorised according to:

1   The type of equipment, for example:
    • audio equipment
    • ergonomic equipment
    • visual equipment.

2   The type of disability it helps, for example:
    • blind/visual
    • cognitive/learning difficulties
    • deaf/hearing
    • dyslexia/specific learning difficulties
    • manual dexterity problems
    • mobility impairments
    • speech impairments.

3   The type/place of use, for example:
    • laboratory work
    • examinations
    • fieldwork
    • lectures/large groups
    • tutorials/small groups
    • assignments
    • research
    • work placement.

Such is the range of products that it is impossible to undertake a review. However, the following types are those most widely used within HE establishments:

- alternatives to a standard keyboard;
- alternatives to a standard mouse;
- screen magnifiers;
- intelligent scanners;
- those which help with speed and accuracy;
- voice recognition;
- voice synthesisers;
- Braille embossers;
- screen readers.

Within each of these groups there may be a number of options available to the disabled student. For example, for some people, typing in general, or specific keyboard skills such as holding down two keys at a time, may be difficult or impossible. Although this may appear to be a relatively serious problem, adapted keyboards can accommodate many difficulties. For example, keyboards can:

- be adapted for use with one hand;
- have enlarged/smaller keypads;
- be 'tuned' so that they react less quickly, for people who dwell a little on each keystroke;
- be used with software which holds down the shift and other control keys;
- be designed for the most comfortable location for the user (e.g. on the arm of a wheelchair);
- be adapted for use with a 'stick' held in the mouth, or other device.

In the UK, there are a number of organisations offering information and advice on technologies to disabled people in general, such as Ability-Net (www.abilitynet.org.uk), or to students in particular, such as TechDis (www.techdis.ac.uk) – most of these are based at universities (but their published advice is available worldwide). Having such organisations as a resource has made it much easier for disabled students to discover possible solutions to their problems. Up until a few years ago it was up to the individual to gather (often biased) information from the relevant manufacturers, whereas now a single organisation can provide all the information. For example, the Technologies for Disabilities Information Service (TechDis) offers an online Accessibility Database (TAD) that reviews over 2500 items of assistive technology used to support disabled students (www.niad.sussex.ac.uk).

Modern ICT gives the disabled student new options and possibilities. However, despite all the information available to the disabled student, there are still pitfalls. For a start, nothing removes the disability itself, and disabled students need to be realistic about what the technology will be able to do for them, and how well it will achieve it. Whatever the disability, and however straightforward the answer may appear to be, it is essential that good independent advice is obtained to ensure that the correct choices are made and the needs of the individual have been best met, before a purchase is made.

Professional needs assessments are now widely available and are essential if the student is applying for a Disabled Students' Allowance (DSA) to cover the costs. However, until the disabled student has personal experience of a range of technologies it is often not possible to know which is the most appropriate. Even if the right technology is chosen, most alternative and adapted technologies need training, time, patience and perseverance before they can be mastered. It is therefore advisable that, unless there is a need for 'standard' equipment, disabled students wait until they have started their studies before applying for a DSA and having an assessment. This gives the disabled student time to try out equipment either at the university, or at another centre which specialises in alternative and adapted technologies; this avoids purchase of equipment which is either too complicated to master or does not do the job for which it is intended.

BARRIERS

Legislation to remove discrimination against disabled people in education and advances in ICT have meant that disabled students are now far more likely to be given the opportunity of using computer and communications technologies (and thus enabling them to undertake HE studies) than ever before. However, despite this progress, there remain barriers that may prevent the disabled student from being able to use the technologies most appropriate to their needs and studies. The main two barriers are 'accessibility' and 'funding'.

Accessibility

Accessibility covers not only whether disabled students have the opportunity to use equipment/software adapted to meet their needs (either by owning it themselves or at the HE establishment), but also whether standard communication tools such as web pages and the Internet are as accessible to disabled as they are to non-disabled students.

Assistive Technology Centres
Until very recently, the only way, as a disabled student, I could use alternative and adapted technology was if I owned this myself. Advice

organisations, such as AbilityNet and the National Bureau for Students with Disabilities (SKILL), offered general advice; but individual universities had relatively little support for the ICT needs of disabled students. It was up to each student to research the possibilities, and to find funding for both an assessment and the equipment. The consequence was that many hours were spent trying to learn how to use equipment or software with no back-up, and no real way of knowing if what one had purchased was the most appropriate.

Today's HE students have much more practical advice available to them. Universities now provide a range of special facilities for users with disabilities and new legislation means that this can only get better. Universities must publish information on facilities for education and research with respect to disabled persons; this also means that disabled students can select one that provides facilities to meet their needs. SKILL has a database of HE establishments that allows prospective students to identify those meeting their needs (e.g. those which already have Brailling facilities) (SKILL 2003a).

Assistive technology centres or departments are relatively recent additions to the IT facilities in HE establishments. Just a few years ago the only special facilities provided were likely to be a lift to the IT department and facilities for students with visual difficulties. These services were typically: the provision of enlarged photocopies; and a workstation which had a screen magnifier, HAL voice synthesiser, Braille printer and flat-bed scanner. A typical higher education establishment now provides various assistive technology packages and related hardware, such as:

- large screen monitors;
- intelligent scanners;
- equipment and screen magnification software, such as 'Zoomtext';
- adjustable workstations and alternative keyboards;
- software for students with dyslexia;
- Braille embossers;
- screen readers which scan books or electronic text aloud, such as 'Kurzweil';
- software to help with note-taking, essay structure, spelling and word definition, visual planning/organising (electronic mind-mapping), such as 'Inspiration';
- voice recognition software, such as 'Dragon Dictate'.

In addition, assistive software, such as 'Texthelp Read and Write' (software to assist with reading and writing), 'Inspiration' (a visual organising tool) and Lunar (screen magnification software) may be networked within the HE institution; and some equipment, such as portable induction loop systems, may be available on loan (Campbell 2003; Southampton Institute 2003a).

Assistive technology centres are usually only accessible to disabled students, and support staff are usually on hand to provide training and support. The equipment in assistive technology centres is purchased by the higher education establishment and is usually updated annually. Many HE libraries also have open access to supportive technology such as Braille embossers, large monitors and video magnifiers.

Internet

The Internet is the fastest growing communications medium ever and has the potential to offer access to information for all. The most obvious advantage to disabled students is the accessibility to a vast amount of information relevant to their studies, and for me, as a Ph.D. research student, access to online databases and websites was essential to the success of my research.

However, despite improved access to information for disabled students due to the World Wide Web, it has been recognised by those involved both in website design and education (Bryne 2001; NDT 2003), that although 'equal access to the Internet in our schools, colleges and universities is of paramount importance' (Bryne 2001, p. 1) there remain many barriers for disabled students which prevent this ideal of 'equal opportunity for all'. The main reason is that, if every student had physical access to computers and including appropriate access technology (e.g. adapted keyboards, large screens, voice synthesisers), large amounts of the World Wide Web would still remain inaccessible to students with physical and/or sensory impairments. It has been estimated that as many as three out of every four websites are inaccessible to disabled people (Bryne 2001), which suggests that disabled students may be severely disadvantaged.

All Web users experience access problems (e.g. when websites use technology/software not installed on one's personal computer, or the user does not have the most recent browser release). However, additional problems exist for disabled people which are more than just a 'nuisance', and can make access to sites impossible. Although it is natural to assume that blind or visually-impaired students would endure the most problems, accessibility problems also occur for students with other disabilities.

One of the main problems encountered by disabled surfers is the tools used to navigate sites. Blind and visually-impaired people often use software which reads the web page aloud using a computer-generated voice. No software is able to 'read' pictures, and so problems occur when graphics (common ones being a 'hand' or a 'pointing finger') are used to indicate how the Web user should move to the next page, or to another part of a site. Inconsistent or complicated navigation schemes can also cause problems for those with learning difficulties, as well as those who have motor or physical impairments. In these cases, something other than a mouse (such as an adapted keyboard or joystick) may be used to interact with the computer. However, websites do not accommodate alternative input devices.

In order to avoid problems such as those mentioned above, websites may now be designed in accordance with:

- guidelines set by the World Wide Web Consortium's (W3C) Web Accessibility Initiative (WAI) (known as the WAI's Web Content Accessibility Guidelines);
- the Centre for Applied Special Technology's BOBBY (BOBBY is an online tool that may be used to test the accessibility of a web page. It may be found at www.cast.org/bobby/).

According to Rowland (2000), lack of access to the Web for disabled students has been recognised as an important issue in the USA, since it limits the students' ability to gather basic course information, conduct research, participate in assignments and so on. She goes on to say that studies at the beginning of the 2000s indicated that BOBBY would approve only about one in four websites commonly used for post-secondary education in the USA, and she believes the situation in the UK to be not dissimilar.

Thus, although information technology has opened up higher education to disabled students for whom access may otherwise have been denied, there remain many inequalitites in its use when compared with non-disabled users. As websites become increasingly sophisticated, and such technology is used globally on such a large scale, it is important to try and remove some of these inequalities if disabled students are to go on to have equal opportunities in the workplace. This is a problem which has been recognised worldwide. According to Bryne (2001), in countries outside of the UK, including the USA and Australia, legislation has been used by disabled people who have been unable to access websites, thus raising awareness of the problem.

Accessibility is increasingly being recognised as a major consideration in the design process of new sites. In the UK, the Special Educational Needs and Disability Act 2001 and Part IV of the DDA, which came into force on 1 September 2002, included requirements that HE establishments' websites must be made accessible. The Act also requires that HE establishments should anticipate adjustments that need to be made, rather than wait until a disabled student asks, for example, that the intranet be made accessible (Corlett 2002). Thus steps are being taken to eliminate some of the discrimination.

Funding

Access to alternative and adaptive ICT at the time that I was undertaking research as a postgraduate student was totally reliant on the financial status of the student, since there was only a very limited range available through the HE establishment itself. Despite the above section demonstrating how general access to alternative and adaptive technologies by disabled students has increased greatly over the past few years, most disabled students will still need to actually own it themselves, or will benefit from doing so. It is unlikely that the individual needs of one disabled student will ever be exactly the same as another, and there are many instances when the disabled student needs to be able to use equipment/software outside of the HE establishment. For example, the disabled student may:

- not find the HE environment comfortable to work in;
- live away from the HE establishment;
- only be able to work for short periods at a time, and cannot easily keep returning to the assistive technology centre;
- need to work outside the assistive technology centre's opening hours;
- need equipment/software which is unavailable at the HE establishment;
- find access to a popular piece of equipment (used on a 'first come first served' basis) is limited.

In these circumstances, and indeed in general, it is far more convenient for the disabled student to have access to a PC and alternative and adaptive technologies at home, in which case the disabled student needs to obtain funding in order to purchase it.

Disabled Students' Allowance

The main source of funding for specialist equipment in England and Wales for those with a disability or specific learning difficulty comes in the form of a Disabled Students' Allowance (DSA). The mandatory regulations do not define 'disability', but allow Local Education Authorities (LEAs) to consider all cases where extra costs are incurred by the student because of mental or physical impairment.

The allowance is available to undergraduates and postgraduates as well as to Open University (OU) and other distance learning students. DSAs used to be available only to full-time students, but since 1 September 2000, part-time students studying the equivalent of at least 50 per cent of a full-time course may also apply, thus opening up opportunities to many disabled people whose disability prevents them from attending a full-time HE course. DSAs are not income-related or means-tested and, unlike a student loan, do not have to be repaid. LEAs may pay DSAs to part-time and full-time undergraduates and certain postgraduates. The OU handles DSAs for their students. The LEA will probably request that a needs assessment is carried out by a person with specialist experience at an independent assessment centre or at the HE establishment. The cost of the assessment can be covered by the DSA (DFES 2002a).

There are three types of DSA available, one of which is specifically for the purchase of specialist equipment (the Specialist Equipment Allowance). This allowance may be used to purchase disability-related specialist equipment to support the disabled student's studies (e.g. personal computer or laptop, specialist furniture, scanners, dictaphones and mini-disc recorders, specialist hardware and software, repair and technical support costs, insurance and extended warranty costs). The LEA (or OU) can also reimburse costs of renting equipment if this is more economical than buying.

A disabled student may apply for a DSA at any point during his or her HE course. In many cases it may be prudent for students to wait until they have started their course before deciding what equipment they need. However, from the academic year 2002/03 once eligibility has been established, i.e. the LEA has accepted proof of the student's disability or a specific learning disability, the LEA can arrange for a needs assessment to be carried out well before the beginning of term (DFES 2002a).

Research councils
Postgraduate students may be able to obtain funding similar to DSAs through the research council which is funding their studies. As each research council has its own proceedure, the student support staff at the relevant council should be contacted by the disabled student.

Hardship (Access) Fund
The Student Hardship Fund or 'Access Fund' is a limited amount of money which is allocated to HE establishments by the government to assist full-time and part-time students who face financial difficulties which may prevent them from accessing HE or completing their studies. Disabled students 'whose disability prevents them from studying 50 per cent of a full-time course' will also be eligible as long as they are studying 25 per cent of a full-time course. Disabled students who have additional expenses which are not covered by the DSA, or those who are not eligible for the allowance, may apply for financial assistance through the fund (DFES 2002a; Southampton Institute 2003b).

Other funding

If disabled people are unable to obtain the money they need from official sources, one option open to them is to apply to trusts and charities to try and raise the funds. Some trusts only help students with disabilities, others help disabled students among other groups. Each trust has its own strict criteria for whom it will help and there are no guarantees that even if a disabled student meets the criteria, he or she will receive any monetary help. Applications need to be:

- tailored to the trust;
- clear about what the money is for;
- realistic;
- sent to meet the deadline – some trusts award money only once or twice a year.

A list of the trusts which are known to help students with disabilities may be obtained from SKILL (SKILL 2003b).

Advances in ICT, aided by recent legislation, have made higher education much more accessible to the disabled person in the UK in recent years. However, unless there are major changes, the two main barriers – 'accessibility' and 'funding' – which prevent equal opportunities in the use of ICT between disabled and non-disabled students, are likely to remain.

Physical access to computers and the Internet are basic requirements for all HE students if they are to take advantage of the new opportunities offered by these technologies. Part IV of the DDA should produce more commitment by HE establishments to providing specialist resources and associated staff training, thus reducing discrimination against disabled students. However, under the new legislation, HE establishments in the UK may have to provide specialist equipment for disabled students only if it is not obtainable via DSAs or other funding. Thus there appears to be a real danger that rather than catering for the disabled student, HE establishments may only do so if the law demands it, i.e. if a disabled person wants to attend, but is prevented from doing so by the lack of specialist ICT equipment/funding available to them. Any provision of assistive ICT equipment will naturally require investment, and faced with the prospect of having to make adjustments to the physical environment of all HE establishments (i.e. access to all buildings and so on) by 1 September 2005 (in order to comply with the DDA: Part IV), it appears unlikely that most will provide more assistive ICT equipment than necessary.

The investment that HE establishments will have to make in order to comply with Part IV of the DDA means that it is essential for them to recruit more disabled people in order to maximise their investment. This could be done in two ways:

1 By giving more publicity to the availability of DSAs – the HEFCE disability performance indicator suggested that only 1.4 per cent of full-time undergraduates applied for support through DSAs (SKILL 2002), whereas HESA figures for 2000/01 suggest that 5 per cent of full-time undergraduates were disabled (HESA 2003a).
2 By promoting the assistive ICT equipment that the HE establishment does provide through Disability Statements and publicity material, and by making sure all students and prospective students are aware of any disability support available.

Otherwise there will remain sectors of higher education, such as medicine, education and music, which attract few, if any, disabled people (SKILL 2002). It should be noted that the HEFCE Disability Performance Indicator showed that fifteen higher education insitutions had zero disabled students (SKILL 2002).

In conclusion, the DDA: Part IV has forced those in HE establishments to examine the needs of the disabled student, and a Quality Assurance Group (DFES 2003) and a Disability Performance Indicator (SKILL 2002) have been established to assess and monitor standards associated with the meeting of these needs. However, if there are to be equal opportunities for disabled students, then their ICT needs must be taken into account at the design stage, rather than by trying to adapt something which is already in existence. For example, as the use of online course materials increases, adopting minimum standards for web design should be a priority.

Disabled people have (however unintentionally) been discriminated against, and segregated from the general population, for too long. As HE establishments are legally obliged under the DDA: Part IV to make adjustments over the next few years, perhaps they should take this opportunity to look at how they can meet the ICT needs of the disabled student, without isolating them from other course members. Of course there is a need for separate specialist assistive technology centres, but the time has come to consider whether some assistive technologies can be offered as an option to all students, rather than an added (and usually expensive) extra for the disabled student. For example, a programme which reads out loud may be all that a visually-impaired student needs to access online course materials. However, while non-disabled students have a choice as to where they study, as well as the option of working together, the disabled student may have to go to a different part of the campus or even go home to work alone. It is important, therefore, for HE establishments to understand that discrimination comes in many guises, and that the key to the future of ICT in higher education must be 'integration' rather than 'segregation'. Otherwise, other forms of discrimination may unwittingly be introduced.

REFERENCES

AbilityNet (2003) *Introduction to Alternative and Adaptive Technology.* AbilityNet. Available at www.abilitynet.org.uk/content/alt_technol/intro/introduction. htm (accessed February 2004).

Bryne, J. (2001) 'Are disabled students set to lose out in the digital revolution?' Available at www.connections.gcal.ac.uk/JimsGuid/AccessToEducation.html (accessed February 2004).

Campbell, L. (Lorna Campbell@solent.ac.uk) (14 March 2003) *Assistive Technology at Southampton Institute.*

Corlett, S. (2002) 'The special education needs and disability act'. *Access denied? Web accessibility and the law.* Information Systems Services, University of Leeds. Available at www.campus.leeds.ac.uk/guidelines/accessibility/ (accessed February 2004).

Curtis, P. (2002) 'Disabled students less likely to go to University'. *Education Guardian* online. Available at EducationGuardian.co.uk/higher news/ (accessed February 2004).

DFES (2002a) *Bridging the Gap: A Guide to the Disabled Students' Allowances (DSAs) in Higher Education 2002/03.* DFES.

DFES (2003) 'Disabled Student Allowance Quality Assurance Group'. *Student Support.* DFES. Available at www.dfes.gov.uk/studentsupport/dsa_.shtml (accessed February 2004).

Disability Resource Centre (2002) 'Disability Discrimination Act Part IV: Education'. University of Cambridge. Available at www.cam.ac.uk/ Cambuniv/disability/senda (accessed February 2004).

HESA (2003a) 'First year UK domiciled HE students by level of course, mode of study, gender and disability'. *Student Tables.* HESA. Available at www.hesa. ac.uk/holisdocs/pubinfo/student/disab01.htm. (accessed February 2004).

HESA (2003b) 'First year UK domiciled HE students by level of course, mode of study, gender and disability'. *Student Tables.* HESA. Available at www.hesa. ac.uk/holisdocs/pubinfo/student/disab45.htm (accessed February 2004).

Luxford, S. (Sara.Luxford@solent.ac.uk) (13 March 2003) *Re: ICT and Disabled Students.*

National Disability Team (NDT) (2003) 'Accessibility statement'. Available at www.natdisteam.ac.uk (accessed February 2004).

NFAC (2003) www.nfac.org.uk (accessed February 2004).

Rowland, C. (2000) 'Accessibility of the Internet in post secondary education: meeting the challenge'. Cited in Bryne (2001).

SENDA (2001) '2001 Chapter 10', in *Special Educational Needs and Disability Act 2001.* The Stationery Office. Available at hmso.gov.uk/acts/acts2001/ 20010010.htm (accessed February 2004).

SKILL (2002) 'Results of the new HEFCE disability performance indicator'. Press Release, 18 December 2002. SKILL. Available at www.skill.org.uk/press/archives/181220022.asp (accessed February 2004).

SKILL (2003a) *Into Higher Education.* SKILL. Available at www.skill.org.uk/into_he/index.asp (accessed February 2004).

SKILL (2003b) *Funding for Disabled Students in Higher Education.* SKILL. Available at www.skill.org.uk/info/infosheets.asp (accessed February 2004).

Southampton Institute (2003a) *Information for Students with Disabilities.* SI. Available at www.solent.ac.uk/welfare/disability/pdf (accessed February 2004).

Southampton Institute (2003b) 'Financial assistance and support'. *Student Support and Welfare.* LIS Learning Support. Available at www.solent.ac.uk/welfare/disability/default.asp?level1id=2743 (accessed February 2004).

TechDis (2003) *TechDis Accessibility Database.* TechDis. Available at www.niad.sussex.ac.uk (accessed February 2004).

TechDis (2003) *Welcome to the TechDis website.* TechDis. Available at www.techdis.ac.uk/ (accessed February 2004).

UK Centre for Legal Education (2003) 'Special Education Needs and Disability Act 2001' (online). University of Warwick. Available at www.ukle.ac.uk/directions/issue4/senda.html (accessed February 2004).

UK Government (2003) *Disability Discrimination Act 1995* (online). The Stationery Office. Available at www.hmso.gov.uk/ (accessed February 2004).

10

e-Mentoring

Jane Field

SUMMARY

A number of educational institutions have developed the use of online or e-Mentoring in recent years. This chapter looks at mentoring generally; e-conversations; ways in which e-Mentoring has been implemented in practice; raises some of the issues about using e-Mentoring, and considers how e-Mentoring can be developed in the future. As with any use of ICT within education, implementing an e-Mentoring arrangement requires training, structures and review in order to ensure a high quality service, which is also addressed within the chapter.

MENTORING

In late 2000, Seaman noted that most staff development tends to involve groups of people and a trainer, but 'when it comes to improving motivation, self-confidence and staff retention, nothing beats coaching and mentoring'. She defines a mentor as 'someone who acts as *your own personal* guide, supporter and advisor'.

Fullerton (1996) has discussed the benefits and approaches of mentoring, and has described a number of different models and definitions of the ways in which the mentor/mentee relationship is offered. Many of the mentoring models used in educational institutions have been adapted from business, where mentoring relationships have been in use for longer than in education. Fullerton suggests that educational institutions are now formalising the concept of mentoring relationships, which have existed in other guises over many years; 'what is new is the recognition, status and value attributed to the process and the benefits which accrue from it.'

Mentoring can provide support, discussion and review of many issues. Mentoring helps:

- people to see things in a different light
- increase and improve self-awareness
- raise awareness of other options and choices
- transfer knowledge and experience
- communication at a number of levels
- interpersonal skills
- time management
- develop insight
- develop a willingness to take risks
- increase confidence and self-esteem.

Another benefit of mentoring is that it can cross disciplines and hierarchies, opening up new ideas through 'cross-fertilisation' of discussion and knowledge. Successful mentoring needs:

- careful planning
- clear goals
- preparation
- implementation and regular contact
- evaluation and review
- a support centre or coordinator.

As such, mentoring is not a cheap option since it requires resources in terms of both development and maintenance; although once successfully implemented, it can provide substantial benefits for both the mentor and the 'mentee'. Some of the benefits to mentees have been outlined above. Mentors have found that mentoring encourages them to review and reflect on their own approaches to work, and to consider how and why they work as they do.

Companies have been using mentoring for a number of years, often as a 'fast-track' for up-and-coming staff whom they wish to groom for management (Clutterbuck, 1994). In higher education, universities have been using mentoring as an additional resource to support staff, particularly new lecturers; for example, the University of Ulster included mentoring as one of the core elements of the Postgraduate Certificate in University Teaching, compulsory for all new lecturers.

E-CONVERSATION

With the advent of email a new and more informal method of communication began to be increasingly used. At the end of the 1980s I remember attending a staff development afternoon at the University of East Anglia on using email; and yet I did not make regular use of this then 'new' form of relatively cheap and (within universities at any rate) accessible communication system. It was not until we ran an international conference for those working in the field of ICT a couple of years later that the benefits of using a universal communication system that overcame the constraints of different time zones and expensive international telephone calls prompted us to begin to actively use email. Almost two decades on, this seems almost laughable, as I, in common with many others, must spend in excess of an hour a day using email as a quick, generally reliable way of communicating at many levels.

Of course, the Internet does not simply provide the tools for communicating on a one-to-one basis. List servers, personal lists, and a range of software programs make it possible to communicate with a number of people at the same time. Many have found that list servers, where postings arrive in the email-box, have a greater success than when using systems such as First Class or Lotus Notes, unless the target group is committed to the online discussion. A disadvantage of list servers is that participants can become frustrated when discussions on a topic 'go on too long', 'become political' or 'digress from the point', while others still feel that the debate is worth continuing. Efficient management of the list server can resolve this. Another frustration with list servers is that too often people send personal replies in response to a query to the whole list, rather than taking the time to send the mail to an individual addressee.

On the other hand, effective list servers can facilitate quality debate, which depending on the membership allows for cross-fertilisation of ideas from people involved in different disciplines and coming from different perspectives. In the past year the NIACE Lifelong Learning mailing list has discussed topics including widening participation, teaching basic ICT skills, definitions of lifelong learning, arts in community development, and mentoring. One of the ways to attempt to alleviate frustrations is to agree on a form of 'netiquette' – i.e. to agree a few basic principles such as using the correct subject heading, sending personal mail to an individual (rather than hitting the group reply button) and keeping contributions to a reasonable length (someone I know expects all emails to be no more than three lines long; while this is rather pedantic, it does make you think about the content of any message sent to her).

Many people working on EU-funded projects attempted to use specific software for project correspondence and discussion (First Class, Lotus Notes, e-groups). Of the projects that I have evaluated and participated in, it has been very difficult to generate regular conversation within these systems. When questioned as to why project members do not make pro-active use of the specialised web-based software the most common reason given is that it is easier to send a message by email rather than to do an additional 'click' to receive or send a contribution on specific systems. However, project participants do find a benefit in using specific web software to send and receive documents and reports pertinent to the project, but stress that everyone should participate, since one of the biggest frustrations is when only a few use the system.

Add to this the development of 'web-zines', message boards, chat rooms and online trading; quite simply, the fact that e-conversation and communication are commonplace for many is inescapable.

ONLINE COMMUNITIES

Online communities are increasing in number. Typing 'online communities' into the Google search engine produced 3,180,000 options in February 2003; this is an increase of over one-third on when the same exercise was carried out less than three years ago. A web-based community is one where individuals with a common interest use ICT as a tool for communication with each other, and a willingness to share knowledge and experiences. The web-based community as a whole may comprise numerous smaller communities with narrower and more specific common interests. As early as 1993, Rheingold could see opportunities for the development of online communities: 'Virtual communities are social aggregations that emerge from the Net when enough people carry on public discussions, long enough and with enough human feeling, to form webs of personal relationships in cyberspace.'

Online communities succeed when they are well coordinated, are of interest to the participants, actively engage members and are moderated. Kim (2000) argues that online communities are 'much the same' as those in the real world, but that they offer 'special opportunities and challenges . . . eras[ing] boundaries created by time and distance . . . mak[ing] it dramatically easier for people to maintain connections, deepen relationships and meet like-minded souls'. At the same time, she does acknowledge that a number of prerequisites and considerable work by the online community leader are required to develop and sustain a lively online community.

Online communities have been used increasingly within education, both formally and informally. Pupils in schools may have been exposed to opportunities to participate in online communities; for example, Think.com (web-enabled software designed and built by Oracle for pupils aged 9 to 19 years and teachers), Schoolmaster, First Class and Digital Brain have entered the market competing for business within the education sector. Most people in the further and higher education sector will have experienced membership of a formal or relatively informal online community and will have their own stories to tell of the effectiveness, or otherwise, of these experiences.

The issues raised with regard to the increasing acceptance and use of the Web for conversation and debate are relevant in terms of the emergence of e-Mentoring. *Working Towards E-Quality in Networked E-Learning in Higher Education* (Beaty *et al.*, 2002) states that networked e-learning 'offers the potential for dialogue with a broader range of people and in a form which allows different styles and preferences to be supported'. The second part of this chapter looks at the potential for e-Mentoring to be part of the e-learning portfolio.

E-MENTORING

The use of e-Mentoring is relatively new; and the development of e-Mentoring has not been without its difficulties. In 2000, Seaman wrote that 'Virtual mentoring is the new buzzword'. She also stated: 'email can remove certain perceptions, assumptions, and prejudices that can occur in human interactions. How will this assist the learning (and mentoring) process?' (Seaman, 2000).

One of the greatest advantages of e-Mentoring, also known as telementoring, cybermentoring or virtual mentoring, is that it offers a very flexible communication environment independent of time and space, allowing for asynchronous exchanges. Mingail (2002) stated that 'e-Mentoring is especially suited to working professionals as it enables a mentoring relationship to exist without the individuals involved having to work in the same office, city or even country. As well, valuable insight and information can be shared without taking too much time out of a busy work schedule.' However, while this may be attractive to both the mentor and the mentee, considerable planning and sustained support need to be available in order to implement a high-quality mentoring programme.

e-Mentoring differs in some ways from traditional mentoring:

- communication is via email and can be relatively instant, and may be more convenient for both mentor and mentee
- mentors and mentees can communicate more easily during the working day

- monitoring procedures may differ
- relationships may be time-bound
- there is greater opportunity to reflect on what has been said before responding.

What is the potential for e-Mentoring within further and higher education? e-Mentoring may be used by staff development teams internally (e.g. with new lecturers or as an element of an internal staff development programme). e-Mentoring may also be offered as a compulsory or optional element to students on distance learning courses (or for that matter any course). It may be used with potential university students, or for students to communicate with people in business and industry prior to making a career choice. It is possible for any lecturer or student to have an e-Mentor located anywhere in the world.

Before establishing an e-Mentoring system there are a range of questions to be addressed. In addition to taking on board the issues pertinent to developing any mentoring support service (addressed earlier in the chapter), there are additional factors specific to implementing online mentoring relationships. These include:

- What constraints are there in using e-Mentoring?
- Will the 'anonymity' of the virtual environment aid or hinder online mentoring?
- Will e-Mentoring be more removed, more objective or more honest?
- Are some issues more 'mentorable' online than others and can e-Mentoring provide personal support or is the focus more knowledge- and skills-based?
- Do questions need to be more focused in an online mentoring relationship?
- Is active two-way conversation possible?

When establishing an e-Mentoring programme, consideration should be given to whether the mentoring will take place on conventional email, or whether alternative software will be used. There is no reason, unless some form of group e-Mentoring is implemented, as to why standard email communication should not be used (which overcomes software installation and access issues).

e-Mentoring guidelines should be developed. These might include:

- the aim of the e-Mentoring programme
- the role of the e-Mentor
- the commitment of the mentor and the mentee
- the regularity of communication between mentor and mentee
- issues that may/may not be addressed

- building in regular opportunities for review
- procedures for use should problems occur
- contact details of the e-Mentoring programme coordinator
- the criteria for measuring success.

These guidelines also form the basis of the learning contract between the mentor and mentee. The coordinator may be responsible for matching mentors and mentees; or mentees may be given the alternative to ask someone if they would be willing to be a mentor. If the latter option is chosen, it is helpful to provide mentees with brief guidelines to choosing their mentor (for example, it is often best to ask someone to whom they are not directly responsible; a shared subject interest is the most common basis on which mentees choose their mentor, or someone who has a number of networks – internal and external – which are a source of information and contacts).

As with any mentoring structure, mentors need to be trained. The induction workshop should address not only the aims of the mentoring programme and the role of the mentor, but also how to effectively engage mentees in the e-Mentoring process. Issues such as the barriers (perceived or real) to using email or web software for mentoring, and the use of language in email (which is often more brief, and sometimes more liable to misunderstanding than other forms of communication) need to be discussed. It may also be appropriate to spend a couple of weeks in 'role-play'; providing the opportunity for the e-Mentor to try out mentoring online before working in partnership with a 'real' mentee.

If it is possible, there is value to be gained from inviting potential mentees to a short workshop on the aims and objectives of the mentoring programme, to give advice about selecting a mentor and to explain the learning contract.

In addition, a clear review structure needs to be built in which will be more frequent during the early days of the programme. The review may take place as a group session with the mentors, which not only allows for a review of what is working well and where the key challenges lie, but also provides an opportunity for the mentors to discuss how the programme is working, and identify common issues that may have arisen.

Much of the literature states that both mentors and mentees benefit from the mentoring experience; mentors benefit from the opportunity to reflect not only on the issues posed by the mentee, but also on their own work. Most mentors also state that they enjoy the experience and are pleased to be able to help. The benefits to mentees, apart from gaining new knowledge and having a 'short cut' to gaining answers to their questions, are that they often gain motivation and encouragement from their mentor, have access to new networks, and that they can try out ideas with someone in a safe environment. Both mentors and mentees generally report that participation in a mentoring programme has supported their own professional development.

Solihull College developed an e-Mentoring service in 2001 as a follow-up to a two-day course on coaching for tutors. The primary aim of the e-Mentoring element was to provide additional support for those tutors (both internal and from other colleges) when undertaking assignments. California State University offers an e-Mentoring service in which university mentors (including both staff and students) are matched with students, teachers and parents from junior high schools and junior colleges. Topics may include discussions on an academic subject, academic counselling or personal counselling. The University of Warwick identified a number of alumni as mentors to mature students in order to support them in making final career choices. The mentors themselves had been mature students, and could thus empathise with the mentees, while at the same time being able to offer both practical advice and experience. A number of colleges and universities participating in the EU Leonardo da Vinci Mobility programme have implemented an e-Mentoring support service for students on placement.

The assumption may be that mentoring always involves a one-to-one relationship. In 2000, a group e-Mentoring approach was piloted to provide professional development for teachers through e-Mentoring. This was developed in response to recent policy developments in the UK and beyond which have greatly strengthened the role of IT as a medium of instruction in schools.

During 2000 and 2001 a group of teachers and others involved with lifelong learning, funded by Oracle and Compaq, using Think.com, developed an alternative approach to one-to-one, face-to-face mentoring. The hypotheses tested were: first, the extent to which e-Mentoring can support professional development; and second, the value of a small team of mentors working together in a private online learning community to respond to mentees' issues and concerns.

The e-Mentoring service provided an online opportunity for teachers to network and share the challenges of using ICT effectively in the classroom. The online dimension facilitated mentoring, by allowing teachers to communicate with one another in an open but structured manner. As an online community it also allows teachers to participate in online discussion, which provides added value for those looking to develop online education communities within the classroom.

The mentors were chosen on the basis of their collective and complementary experience in the use of ICT in schools, and all mentors had experience of involvement in online communities. During the Induction Day, the mentors received face-to-face training about the role of the mentor, e-Mentoring and technical practicalities. They also worked together to consider how the online team could best support other teachers. Six months into the programme the mentors met again to review how effective online mentoring had been, good practice, constraints and other issues. The entire process was kept under regular review, with the mentors discussing issues online at regular intervals. It was emphasised throughout that the e-Mentoring service was not viewed as a quick-question, quick-fix or one-way process, but rather as an opportunity for discussion and reflection. All members of the mentoring team would reply to all contributions posed by the mentees.

Mentees were followed up four to five weeks after they left the e-Mentoring community with a view to establishing whether they had implemented anything new as a result of their involvement, or whether they could identify other forms of impact arising from participation in e-Mentoring. The follow-up emails showed that the mentees tried out new ideas, looked at new websites suggested, and thought more about some of the implications of using ICT for teaching and learning.

Originally this group approach had been agreed to prevent any one mentor from being overloaded; but in practice the group approach defined the way in which the community works. The range of experience ensured that the input from the e-Mentors offered a wide perspective and range of ideas in response to all the contributions made on the e-Mentoring community. Furthermore, evidence showed that the e-Mentors not only offered new ideas to the mentees, but that they 'spark off' each other, encouraging further reflection and discussion. The main difficulty experienced during this project was the reluctance of many to enter into ongoing online debates. The e-Mentors agreed to use more phrases that might encourage people to respond and continue a dialogue (e.g. 'Have you thought about/tried/seen/looked at . . . ?'; 'Try and see . . .'; 'Let us know').

Universities have also used a group of mentors rather than the more traditional one-to-one mentoring partnerships. For example, the University of Texas, in partnership with the Texas Center for Educational Technology, used a team of expert mentors as a resource to support the Electronic Emissary Project (EEP), which helps teachers identify experts in different disciplines. The University of Oldenburg (Germany) was involved in a Project to Link Universities and Training Organizations, which developed a European educational network with about eight volunteer teacher mentors to provide mentoring support in their own organisations and across the network. The mentors have different specialist areas which allows them to respond more effectively to queries. At the University of Hawaii they use a mentoring programme to assist newly admitted students. A mentoring team of experienced users responds to questions submitted by students to a list server. Every member of the mentoring team receives the questions, and they take turns in answering questions so as to lower the demands on everyone and to get questions answered quickly. Other mentors may also contribute answers.

The Northeastern University's College of Engineering (US) has an e-Mentoring programme comprising mentoring groups consisting of undergraduate Northeastern University students, professional engineers and high school students. Each group comprises six participants including women in their first year at college, university faculty, professional female engineers and girls still at school. The e-Mentoring experience links participants (e.g. while the undergraduate student will mentor a pre-college student, she, in turn, will be mentored by a working professional).

ISSUES

Due to the lack of signals such as body language, e-Mentors need to be careful to explain what they mean, and avoid making contentious remarks. e-Mentoring is not necessarily anonymous; there has often been some contact between mentors and mentees, either in the past or during the programme, that includes the e-Mentoring element. Some programmes attempt to bring mentors and mentees together at some point.

The opportunities of developing a team of mentors have been raised above. This is different from the traditional notion of mentoring (i.e. a one-to-one relationship); and group e-Mentoring has an advantage over the face-to-face mentoring partnership, since a group of mentors in the flesh could be intimidating. As it is, the collective approach and the mix of the mentors' expertise and various experiences can provide a more rounded discussion from a number of different perspectives. The wider viewpoint and the broad discussions ensure that the mentee is not locked into the view of any one individual. This approach provides mentees with the opportunity to look at issues more widely.

There are quality issues in any mentoring programme, since the mentoring coordinator is not present either during face-to-face mentoring partnerships, or online. It is for this reason that feedback must be sought from both the mentor and the mentee. In addition to regular review, everyone participating in the programme should be aware that there is a support service that can help resolve difficulties, and if necessary change the partnership.

In conclusion, using some of the literature available (on the Web as well as traditional published papers and books), it is possible to identify key elements that support the development of a quality e-Mentoring programme:

- Mentors need support: this can include formal and informal ways to provide feedback, regular reviews, training workshops; opportunities to share experiences and to be able to communicate with each other (e.g. through an online list server).
- Both mentors and mentees should have basic information about the other before they start (a simple form can collect agreed data).
- Mentoring goals should be clearly defined at the outset; this includes identifying the criteria for measuring success.
- Mentoring is not a static activity; as such it may be necessary to adjust the service provided in response to feedback from mentors and mentees.
- The personal interaction (online) between mentor and mentee can determine the effectiveness of the mentoring relationship. Mentors and mentees need to be carefully matched, which is easier when there is an available 'pool' of mentors to choose from, or where mentees choose their own mentor (guidelines can help them in their choice).
- Both mentors and mentees should be clear about the service provided, and its limitations. Agreeing the learning contract and ascertaining expectations beforehand should help to ensure that both parties are aware of what is involved.
- The mentor and mentee need to agree on the extent of their contact. Online communication may be possible on a weekly basis. The learning contract should specify the frequency of communication expected, and also the extent to which the mentor can respond to urgent calls for help or enquiries. Generally, it is regarded as the role of the mentor to initiate contact when there has been a lull in online communication.
- Recognise the contribution made by the mentors; very often they are doing this as an additional activity, and may have volunteered to take part in the programme.

All of us know people with whom we communicate well on email; and we also know those people or those times when it is more productive to use the phone or send a letter. e-Mentoring is not going to suit everyone; but for those who can develop a positive e-Mentoring partnership, or enter into a group mentoring programme, there can be tremendous benefits for everyone involved.

REFERENCES

Beaty, L., Hodgson, V., Mann, S. and McConnell, D. (2002) *Working Towards E-Quality in Networked E-Learning in Higher Education: A Manifesto Statement for Debate*, Dissemination Event, University of Sheffield.

Clutterbuck, D. (1994) Business mentoring in evolution. *Mentoring and Tutoring*, Vol. 2 No. 1.

Field, J. (2001) Ten heads are better than one. *Mentoring News*, spring.

Fullerton, H. (1996) *Facets of Mentoring – Volume 1*, SEDA Paper 94, Birmingham, Staff and Educational Development Association.

Kim, A.J. (2000) *Community Building on the Web*, Berkeley, CA: Peachpit Press.

Mingail, S. (2002) *Law Firm e-Mentoring*, Aurora, Ontario: Canada Law Book Inc.

Rheingold, H. (1998) *The Virtual Community* [online document]. Available at http://www.rheingold.com/vc/book/ (accessed February 2004).

Seaman, J. (2000) An affair that does you good, *The Times Higher Education Supplement*, 1 September.

Wighton, D. *Telementoring: An Examination of the Potential for an Electronic Network, USWEST Fellows and Telementoring*. Available at http://mentor.creighton.edu/htm/telement.htm (accessed February 2004).

11

Networked professional development

Vic Lally and David McConnell

SUMMARY

This chapter considers the emerging role of ICTs in networked professional development. A wide range of strategies for supporting networked professional development (NPD) are considered including the use of online guests, archiving, mixed models of interaction, pairing of participants, personal projects, mentoring and computer-mediated conferences.

INTRODUCTION

Increasingly, computer networks are being used to mediate staff development in higher education institutions (HEIs). Networked support may be appropriate to many areas of staff development, including management and skills development. It is particularly appropriate to provision seeking to support and develop staff use of information and communication technologies (ICTs) in teaching and learning.

Networked professional development for staff takes different forms; there is evidence in the literature reviewed of attempts to match different applications of the technology to different pedagogical purposes. Computer networks also offer opportunities to work across traditional departmental and institutional boundaries, and the increasing practice of collaboration between support staff and academics, and between institutions, reflects this new potential. Such new patterns of provision also indicate a requirement for the acquisition of new skills by staff developers and support staff. These skills include the ability to use computer networks to mediate staff development around ICT, as well as to be able to work online with others. Networked group learning (as we shall refer to the skills required to work with others online) is therefore important for pedagogical and strategic reasons. If networked professional development is to be effective and to become common practice it is clear that staff developers themselves will also need support and professional development provision.

This chapter presents a review of current practice in NPD for networked group learning, based on a survey from around the world. The chapter in this volume by Bowskill and Foster (Chapter 12) will describe and analyse how the findings from this review were used by the Computer Based Collaborative Group Work Project (CBCGW) to build an online course for staff developers. In the final section of this chapter we summarise some of the findings and implications for staff developers of this emerging global networked professional development movement.

OVERVIEW OF CURRENT PRACTICE

In this section of the chapter we look at current practices in support of networked learning that use both traditional and networked strategies. We refer to two surveys:

Survey of off-line support for networked learning

The Talisman project based at Herriot-Watt University in Edinburgh carried out a survey of staff developers in Scottish higher education institutions and asked about the support given to academics for the use of technology in teaching and learning. The report is interesting because the findings may be directly generalisable to other institutions in the UK and will have application elsewhere (Alexander, 1999).

Among the findings in this report were details of two forms of provision using traditional methods. One of these practices was the provision of support for academics to use tools such as email, web browsers, chat systems and other tools (i.e. technical skills). The other form of reported practice was to work with academics to raise their awareness of different technologies and their possible applications.

As a result of these findings, the Talisman report identified a gap in support for pedagogical applications of technology. However, among other comments the report noted that in order for this gap to be filled staff developers might benefit from a forum where ideas and good practices could be shared and discussed. The report also observed that in order to provide support to academics for the pedagogical applications of technology, staff developers may themselves require some support. In addition, we feel that the opportunity to learn about networked learning experientially, by participating in such online events, is of great benefit.

The Computer Based Collaborative Group Work Project (undated) aims to provide a 'training the trainers' initiative for networked group learning. To prepare this in the most appropriate form we carried out our own survey of networked professional development that used group learning activities.

Survey of online support for group learning

We carried out a review of networked staff development practice and drew upon examples from all over the world. All these examples were networked practices using group learning activities. Some of these were entirely online and others also included some face-to-face meetings. The details of this review are provided elsewhere (see Bowskill *et al.*, 1999) and pressures of space here permit only an overview of these practices.

Here, we look at various online strategies for professional development events being offered. Examples range from those aimed at a very well-defined, and sometimes very local audience, to those offered to a highly distributed and changing audience profile.

COLLABORATIVE STRATEGIES FOR ONLINE STAFF DEVELOPMENT EVENTS

A wide range of strategies is used for networked professional development (see Figure 11.1 for an overview). These include:

- use of guests;
- use of archives;
- use of mixed modes of interaction;
- pairing of participants;
- personal projects;
- mentoring/apprenticeships;
- online conferences.

Each of the elements identified above and in Figure 11.1 are discussed briefly in the following paragraphs.

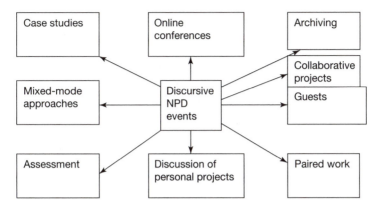

Figure 11.1 *Overview of discursive NPD events*

Guest experts

Particularly prominent in the survey are examples of the use of experts or guests interacting with others in online events. These guests are employed individually or in clusters, and interact with a given audience using a range of tools. There are also examples of experts being involved in a face-to-face setting and online (mixed mode).

The NetLinkS Project brought experienced practitioners into an email-based 'mini-conference' to interact with list members over a three-week period (Levy *et al.*, 1996). A similar approach has been used in a collaborative provision between the University of Sheffield School of Education and the Department of Psychology at the University of Massachusetts, USA (Reilly, 1999). Using an email discussion list, their 'Guest Speaker' series involves a speaker posting a presentation message and then engaging with the list members for a period of seven to ten days. In another example, twenty-three experts from around the world were invited and brought together in a conferencing environment for a forum also lasting three weeks (Anderson and Kanuka, 1997).

In an earlier approach, a virtual seminar was held involving participants from fifteen institutions around the world. The event was organised as a collaboration between the University of Maryland, USA and the University of Oldenburg in Germany (Bernath and Rubin, 1997). The seminar was subdivided into ten units each hosted by a different guest expert. The event was hosted within a conferencing environment, with various support materials offered via the Web. Staff at the University of North Texas were involved in monthly face-to-face meetings where guest experts were invited to make a presentation and discuss their work with participants (Jopling, 1997).

Mixed-mode provision

There is also a range of NPD events that include some form of face-to-face meeting. The use of the face-to-face element varies in different instances. Sometimes it is used to launch an online event; at other times it is used in a series of unit milestones, and at other times as a bridge between self-study and online group discussions.

For instance, staff at the University of Queensland, Australia were offered three themes to explore over a six-week period using an email discussion list (De Vries *et al.*, 1995). Sixty members of staff subscribed to the list. These themes offered a structured exploration of the viability of the network for professional development. In another institutional setting, eleven graduate teaching assistants had weekly face-to-face meetings and the discussions were supported and sustained through the use of a computer conferencing system (Sharpe and Bailey, 1998).

In another example, combining face-to-face and online discussions, participants from different institutions were paired as part of a workshop. The pairs met face-to-face at the beginning of the workshop and then came together with the other pairs at the end of a six-week period to present their findings (Gonzales and Hill, 1997). Staff at the University of Sheffield met face-to-face and were then involved in an online forum lasting ten weeks. This provision was moderated collaboratively between two members of staff. Each week the two moderators provided focus questions to stimulate discussion (Hammond, 1997).

In another example, staff at the UK Open University sent out paper-based open learning materials to address introductory aspects of a short course (Anderson, 1999). A face-to-face meeting followed to develop some of the learning from those materials and to provide training for the use of an online conferencing system. The conferencing system then provided the vehicle for collaborating with others and participating in various online activities. This event lasted for six weeks, with two weeks of self-study followed by four weeks online.

In a final example, the University of Southern Queensland, Australia offered a sixteen-week foundation module divided into five topics. Each topic began with a face-to-face meeting in which materials were offered and discussions held. Thereafter, the activities were all online (Naidu, 1997).

Using archives

The use and reuse of the archive resulting from the online discussion has been valued in a number of instances. Sometimes this archive is left as a stand-alone resource for anyone who has access, sometimes the archive is periodically summarised by moderators, and in other cases it is used as a resource for a follow-up event. In addition, an archive is sometimes re-purposed for a different audience.

In an online workshop for staff developers from institutions around the USA, the sixteen participants worked through five units over an eight-week period and made particular mention of the value and availability of the online archive (Kleiman, 1999). More formal use was made of the archive in another instance, when an online event was revisited using email to explore and discuss the archive and the overall experience (Bernath and Rubin, n.d.). In another example of collaboration between a university and two schools, participants in an online event covered a number of weekly topics (Little-Reynolds and Takacs, 1998). At the end of each topic the moderator provided a detailed summary of the online discussion and the key points arising. These summaries were then gathered into an archive as a resource for the workshop and subsequent review. Finally, an online forum of guest experts was archived and made available to others as a learning resource (Anderson and Kanuka, n.d.).

Case studies

Case studies are also presented in the literature. In one example, participants examined a documented case of a given student and this was then accompanied by providers role-playing different parties in the case study. The exploration of the case was structured over a four-week period and the combination of the case study and the role-playing was seen as very effective in subsequent evaluations (Zorfass *et al.*, 1998).

Pairing participants

There is evidence of several cases where participants in an online event work in pairs. This included mixed-mode activities between different institutions. It also included paired presentations and paired hosting of online discussions.

One example has already been mentioned above where paired tutors and Ph.D. students in different institutions worked together as part of a workshop activity (Gonzales and Hill, 1997). In an American example participants in a mathematics programme were paired over an eight-week period, all of which was online (Tinker and Haavind, 1997). During this period participants were required to host online discussions on teaching strategies or content topics. This event involved twelve participants (all schoolteachers) working in pairs within an online forum. A university hosted the forum. In another example, the moderation of an online event was conducted in pairs (Hammond, 1997).

Personal project development

The development of personal projects in a collaborative event is yet another strategy evidenced in the literature.

One interesting example of this is in the NetLinkS Project at the University of Sheffield, England. In this example, participants from institutions around the UK participated in a sixteen-week course and developed a personal work-related project in collaboration with other participants (Levy *et al.*, 1996). Another example of this may be seen in America where staff at the University of North Texas developed a personal project over the course of one semester (Jopling, 1997). This institutional initiative involved participants in monthly face-to-face meetings where guest experts were invited to make a presentation and discuss their work with participants.

Collaborative projects

The M.Ed. in networked collaborative learning at the University of Sheffield incorporates a variety of collaborative and cooperative group projects.

Collaborative distributed problem-based learning
This is where course participants work in small learning sets to define a problem relating to the practice of networked learning that is amenable to collaborative group work. The purpose of this is to help:

- Participants experientially understand and critically evaluate the nature and complexity of collaborative group work in virtual learning environments. This understanding contributes to the development of their own professional practice in networked learning.
- Participants work collaboratively on a shared problem that will lead to a portfolio outcome which may be shared with other learning sets.
- Each participant critically reflect on the experience using a set of self-analysis tools. The outcome of this critical reflection is then made available to the learning set members, who also offer their 'assessment' of each participant's self-analysis.

Cooperative distributed problem-based learning
This is where individuals within a learning set define an agenda for carrying out a course assignment chosen by themselves in consultation with their peer learners and tutor. This assignment is designed around a real problem or issue that they face in their professional practice (or their organisation faces) which is amenable to being carried out by action

research. The focus of the problem is always around some aspect of networked learning. This form of learning is based on principles of self-managed learning, as well as principles of cooperative learning.

Participants work cooperatively in virtual learning environments such as Lotus Notes and WebCT to help and support each other in:

- Defining the problem and its overall scope.
- Considering its appropriateness as an assignment for their M.Ed. degree which will both illuminate some aspect of problem-based professional practice and also contribute to an understanding of networked learning.
- Offering each other support in finding resources that may be useful in considering theoretical underpinnings for analysing the problem or issue being researched, and in considering the implications for professional networked learning practice.

These group learning strategies are discussed more extensively in McConnell (2000).

Mentoring

There are several examples of participants involved in mentoring others who may have less experience or understanding. This took several forms including one person modelling good practice for others; training others to host an event; people with a particular skill supporting others; and groups of mentors supporting each other.

Some instances of this were mentioned above, for example, where a tutor was paired with a Ph.D. student as part of a workshop (Gonzales and Hill, 1997). There are also other examples that are less structured. The TappedIN project is one instance where those wishing to host an online event at some future date are free to do so, but on condition that they have attended an event hosted by someone else to provide a model of teaching in a real-time event. There was also a similar case at the UK Open University, where a participant in an online course later became a tutor and was invited to help 'cascade' the course to another group (Anderson, 1999). Elsewhere, participants in a programme offered to schools invited each school to identify a volunteer to act as a novice moderator and to support the main moderator while observing some of the skills involved. There are a number of examples of tele-Mentoring (Eisenman and Thornton, 1999; Taylor and Singh, 1997) and of online apprenticeships (Treacy and Johnson, 1999).

The NetLab Project also makes use of this mentoring/apprenticeship strategy in another form. In this example, a number of mentors were appointed and identified to a corresponding set of institutions. This network of available mentors functions as representatives for a cluster of schools. The project networks the mentors as a group and each mentor is able to share experiences and tips to overcome objections elsewhere. In this way each mentor supports his or her own school but also the other mentor (Muscella and Di Mauro, 1995). A variant of this idea of staff developers supporting each other is seen in Sherry's paper on collaborative research (Sherry and Myers, 1996). In this paper the authors describe how they adopted a reflective practice approach to the support of others in the institution, and were thereby able to develop their own skills and knowledge. In a final example under this heading, participants in an online course were each invited to identify and brief an interested volunteer on their campus to participate in the next edition of the course (Hoffman and Ritchie, 1998).

Assessment

There are a number of examples of aspects of assessment being incorporated into professional development provision outside of a formal course. At Central Queensland University, participants were invited to work through six online course units. Each unit modelled a different assessment strategy and each was progressively more difficult than the last (Macpherson *et al.*, 1997). In another example, participants in an online event had the option of submitting a portfolio of evidence for assessment purposes (Sharpe and Bailey, 1998). The M.Ed. in networked collaborative learning at the University of Sheffield involves participants using a variety of collaborative assessment methods. Members of learning sets participate in collaborative (self/peer/tutor) review and assessment procedures where each participant brings a set of criteria which they would like members to use in making judgements about their assignment, in addition to the use of a set of criteria which are offered by the tutor. The review is an opportunity for participants and tutor to read each others' assignment, critically discuss and examine the issues in it, offer insights into the meaning of the assignment as a method for examining the original problem, suggest additional references and resources that might be useful, and finally offer comment on the extent to which the assignment meets the writer's set of criteria and those offered by the tutor (McConnell, 2000).

Online conferences

There are a number of examples of online conferences and, again, there are mixed modes of provision. These include examples where the entire event is online and structured in a broadly similar way to a traditional setting. This is the case in the TCC Annual Online Conference that brings together participants from across the educational sectors including schools, colleges and universities. Various speakers interact with participants from around the world in both delayed and real-time activities. This is restricted to a fee-paying audience and is entirely online.

In a variant an online conference runs in parallel to a traditional conference format. This was seen in the Bangkok Project where all conference papers were placed online for remote participants to discuss the same topics according to their concerns. There were also instances of discussions at the traditional format event being relayed to other lists elsewhere, and responses fed back to the main event (Anderson and Mason, 1993). It was equally possible for the defined face-to-face audience to interact with the remote unknown audience. Aspects of the Bangkok Project have been replicated in another case in Australia where a face-to-face conference was supplemented by an online conference running in parallel (Ivanoff, 1998).

CONCLUSION – NETWORKED PROFESSIONAL DEVELOPMENT: IMPLICATIONS FOR STAFF DEVELOPMENT

In this chapter, we have sought to present a review of current initiatives in networked professional development. The review draws on a worldwide literature and indicates that a wide range of strategies is currently being used in networked professional development. These include the use of guests, archives, mixed modes of interaction, pairing of participants, personal projects, mentoring/apprenticeships and computer-mediated conferences.

These initiatives range from those aimed at well-defined local activities to those offered to a highly distributed and changing audience profile. They indicate a widening interest in the use of ICT for supporting staff development as well as an interest in developing user skills in, and knowledge of, networked learning. These developments have significant implications for staff developers. Increasingly, it will become necessary for those involved in the support and development of academics in higher education to understand the role of computer-mediated teaching and learning in higher education. Furthermore, staff developers will need to acquire in-depth experiential understanding of computer-mediated teaching and learning for themselves if they are to maintain and develop a pivotal role in the dynamic changes occurring in the university sector at the start of the twenty-first century. But the challenge does not end there, since, to make a significant impact on these changes, staff developers will need to get ahead of the game, and mediate the creative translation of research in this field into exciting new approaches to teaching and learning. The alternative to this scenario should be contemplated with care by those who have an interest in the field of staff development in higher education.

REFERENCES

Alexander, W. (1999) *TALiSMAN Review of Staff Development Courses and Materials for C&IT in Teaching, Learning and Assessment.* Available at http://www.talisman. hw.ac.uk/CITreview/cit_index.html (accessed February 2004).

Anderson, K.J. (1999) *Staff Development in Supporting Learning with Technology.* Available at http://icdl.open.ac.uk/lit2k/LitResult.ihtml?&id=18077 (accessed February 2004).

Anderson, T. and Kanuka, H. (n.d.) Online Forums: New Platforms for Professional Development and Group Collaboration. *Journal of Computer Mediated Communication,* 3 (3). Available at http://www.ascusc.org/jcmc/vol3/issue3/anderson.html (accessed February 2004).

Anderson, T. and Mason, R. (1993) The Bangkok Project. *The American Journal of Distance Education,* 7 (2), pp. 5–18.

Bernath, U. and Rubin, E. (n.d.) *Virtual Seminar for International Professional Development in Distance Education.* Available at http://www.umuc.edu/~erubin/article1.html (accessed February 2004).

Bowskill, N., Foster, J., Lally, V. and McConnell, D. (1999) *A Rich Professional Development Environment (RPDE) for University Staff to Explore and Develop Networked Collaborative Learning.* European Conference on Educational Research 1999, Lahti, Finland, 22–25 September.

Computer Based Collaborative Group Work Project (undated). Available at http://collaborate.shef.ac.uk (accessed February 2004).

De Vries, L., Naidu, S., Jegede, O. and Collis, B. (1995) On-line professional staff development: an evaluation study. *Distance Education,* 16 (1), pp. 157–73.

Eisenman, G. and Thornton, H. (1999) Tele-mentoring: helping new teachers through the first year. *T.H.E Journal Online,* April. Available at http://www.thejournal.com/magazine/vault/A2065.cfm (accessed February 2004).

Gonzales, C. and Hill, M. (1997) Faculty from Mars, technology from Venus: mentoring is the link. *Technology and Teacher Education Annual,* pp. 16–20. Formerly available at http://www.coe.uh.edu/insite/elec_pub/HTML1997/fd_gonz.htm.

Hammond, M. (1997) Developing networked learning within higher education: a case study of an electronic forum for university staff. *Teaching in Higher Education,* 2 (3), pp. 243–57.

Hoffman, B. and Ritchie, D. (1998) Teaching and Learning Online: Tools, Templates and Training. *Proceedings of SITE 98 9th International Conference,* Washington, DC, 10–14 March. Formerly available at http://www.coe.uh.edu/insite/elec_pub/HTML1998/de_hoff.htm.

Ivanoff, G. (1998) Running a virtual conference: lessons learned. In C. McBeath and R. Atkinson (eds) *Planning for Progress, Partnership and Profit.* Proceedings EdTech'98. Perth: Australian Society for Educational Technology.

Jopling, J. (1997) *Faculty Training and Support.* Formerly available at http://www. cdlr.tamu.edu/dec/papers/jopling/ jopling. htm.

Kleiman, G. (1999) Online Workshop for Education Leaders. Leadership and the New Technologies. *LNT Perspectives,* Issue 7, January/February. Available at http://www.edc.org/LNT/news/Issue7/feature2.htm (accessed February 2004).

Levy, P., Fowell, S., Bowskill, N. and Worsfold, E. (1996) NetLinks: a national professional development project for networked learner support. *Education for Information,* 14 (4), pp. 261–78.

Little-Reynolds, L. and Takacs, J. (1998) *Distance Collaboration and Technology Integration Between Two Institutions.* Formerly available at http://www.coe. uh.edu/insite/elec_pub/HTML1998/ fd_litt.htm.

Macpherson, C., Bennett, S. and Priest, A. (1997) The DDCE Online Learning Project. *ASCILITE '97 Conference.* Available at http://www.ascilite.org.au/ conferences/perth97/papers/Macpherson/Macpherson.html (accessed March 2003).

McConnell, D. (2000) *Implementing Computer Supported Co-operative Learning.* London: Kogan Page.

Muscella, D. and Di Mauro, V. (1995) *LabNet: An Electronic Forum to Support Teaching Science.* Formerly available online at: http://www.coe.uh.edu/ insite/elec_pub/html1995/076.htm.

Naidu, S. (1997) Collaborative reflective practice: an instructional design architecture for the Internet. *Distance Education,* 18 (2), pp. 257–83.

Reilly, R.A.(1999) EdNet@Umass: Providing Quality Professional Development via the Internet. *T.H.E Journal Online,* March. Available at http://www.the journal.com/magazine/vault/A2098.cfm (accessed February 2004).

Sharpe, R. and Bailey, P. (1998) Networked learning for professional development: design and evaluation of technologies to meet learning outcomes. *Proceedings of Networked Lifelong Learning Conference,* Sheffield University.

Sherry, L. and Myers, K.M. (1996) Developmental research on collaborative design. *Proceedings of the 43rd Annual Conference of the Society for Technical Communication.* Charlottesville, VA: Society for Technical Communication. Available at http://www.cudenver.edu/~lsherry/pubs/dev_research.html (accessed February 2004).

Taylor, J. and Singh, H. (1997) *Globalisation of Professional Development: A Teaching and Learning Perspective.* Formerly available at http://cwis.usq.edu.au/dec/ staff/taylorj/97penn.doc.

Tinker, R. and Haavind, S. (1997) Netcourses and Netseminars: Current Practice and New Designs. *Netcourse Article,* July. Available at http://www.concord.org/ library/pdf/netcours.pdf (accessed March 2003).

Treacy, B. and Johnson, K. (1999) Online Professional Development for Teachers: A Collaborative Model. *Leadership and the New Technologies,* 10, July/August. Available at http://www.edc.org/LNT/news/Issue10/feature2. htm (accessed February 2004).

Zorfass, J., Remz, A. and Ethier, D. (1998) Illustrating the Potential of an Online Workshop through a Case Study Example. *CMC Magazine*, February. Available at http://www.december.com/cmc/mag/1998/feb/zorfas.html (accessed February 2004).

12

Networked staff development: a case study

Nicholas Bowskill and Jonathan Foster

SUMMARY

This chapter describes an initiative to explore current practices and professional development needs among staff developers wishing to introduce a new practice of networked staff development particularly for teaching and learning. A case study of an online short course for staff developers is described and some conclusions are drawn from the findings. The work described is part of the provision and support of the Computer Based Collaborative Group Work Project in the School of Education. Further details of this project along with a review of current practice in networked staff development are described by Lally and McConnell in Chapter 11 of this book.

INTRODUCTION

There is an increasing use of computer networks to deliver staff development in higher education institutions (HEIs). Networked support may be appropriate to many areas of staff development including management and skills development. It is particularly appropriate to provision seeking to support and develop staff use of information and communication technology (ICT) in teaching and learning. Networked staff development (NSD) is a new kind of practice that often involves both participants and providers working within and across institutional boundaries. Just as academic staff are finding their work being redefined by technology (Ryan *et al.*, 2000), so too are library staff (Levy *et al.*, 1996) and staff development providers. A review of networked staff development is provided in Bowskill *et al.* (2000) and here by Lally and McConnell (see Chapter 11, this volume).

The introduction of technology raises serious issues for re-skilling of many people working in higher education (Beaty, 1995). The skills indicated for staff developers include not only the ability to use the networks to deliver staff development around ICT, but also to work online with others in making that provision. Networked group learning is therefore important for pedagogical and strategic reasons. However, if networked staff development is to be effective and to become common practice it is clear that staff developers will also need support and professional development provision (Alexander, 1999).

This chapter describes a survey of UK staff developers carried out in a series of regional workshops to examine current needs and practices for NSD. The chapter goes on to examine an online workshop provided by the project to staff developers as a response to some of the identified needs. Both the survey and the online workshop were delivered as part of the work of the Computer Based Collaborative Group Work (CBCGW) Project. The project was funded by the Higher Education Funding Council for England (HEFCE) as a Phase 3, Teaching and Learning Technology Project (TLTP, undated).

The CBCGW Project involved raising awareness and providing experience and support of networked collaborative learning, and was conceptualised in five related strands:

1   The establishment of a web-based National Professional Development Centre for Computer Based Collaborative Group Work in Higher Education (CBCGW, undated).
2   A case study evaluation of generic online teaching and learning strategies in professional development.
3   The development, research, evaluation and dissemination of a rich professional development environment (RPDE) for university teachers.
4   A study of institutional readiness for networked collaborative learning.
5   A review of group-ware for networked group work.

The project aimed to research and support the development of group learning within a networked environment and a key part focused on staff developers in institutions of higher education.

PROJECT STAFF DEVELOPMENT SUPPORT INITIATIVE

Having completed a sampling of current practice from the literature, we sought to identify some of the current practices and specific needs of UK staff developers. Regional workshops for staff developers were held in London, Edinburgh and Sheffield from February to March 2000. The workshops brought together a total of fifty-six staff developers representing thirty-four different higher education institutions.

In this small survey we sought to answer three questions:

1 What are the current practices of staff developers to support networked learning (with a particular interest in networked experiential strategies)?
2 What are the sources of help used by staff developers to educate themselves in this area?
3 What are the professional development needs of staff developers to be able to deliver networked staff development for group learning?

REGIONAL WORKSHOP FINDINGS

We found that many of the off-line support practices were broadly consistent with the findings reported in the Talisman project report (Alexander, 1999). These activities included working with individual academics, putting on workshops and providing demonstrations. Our survey also found the use of focus groups as a different face-to-face strategy to those mentioned in the Talisman report.

The findings from our regional workshops, relating to *online* practices, were broadly consistent with those in the Talisman survey. We found considerable use of networked resource-based learning as a non-discursive strategy. We also found some evidence of the provision of communication tools (chat systems and conferencing systems) and some online group learning activities as part of a professional development provision.

We also asked staff developers about their sources of help in developing their own understanding of networked learning. The main sources reported included the use of national services such as SEDA or the Teaching and Learning Technology Support Network. In addition, where staff developers also had a TLTP project in their institution they often used any of their available products. Discussion with colleagues was the other main source of support used by staff developers.

It is clear, even from this limited sampling of UK staff developers, that the help available to them to support networked group learning is very informal in nature. It was therefore not surprising that the professional development needs reported by staff developers included a wish for examples of good practice, firsthand experience of networked group learning and more time to digest this new information and consider the implications for their practice. As a response to the identified needs, we sought to provide an online short course for staff developers. The remainder of this chapter describes the online short course and some of the initial findings.

THE ONLINE SHORT COURSE FOR STAFF DEVELOPERS

To provide staff developers with firsthand experience of networked group learning, the project offered an online short course for staff developers interested or involved in support for ICT.

Recruitment and participant profile

Recruitment for the course was organised using traditional and online methods. At each of the three regional workshops, participants were handed a flyer detailing the online course and how to apply. About 25 per cent of those recruited came from one of these workshops. We also sent one email message to each of two mailbase discussion lists (seda @mailbase.ac.uk and staff-development@mailbase.ac.uk) to advertise the course. These lists were selected as being those most relevant to our target audience. The remaining 75 per cent of course participants were recruited as a result of this online strategy.

We offered a total of nineteen places for the online course and charged £50 sterling per person to cover administrative costs and also to encourage participation in the course. In recognition of the potential to work across international as well as institutional boundaries we also accepted three applicants from outside of the UK (one from New Zealand, one from Australia and another from Ireland).

Structure of the short course

The short course was divided into four units and ran for eight weeks. Table 12.1 shows the structure of the course.

Table 12.1 *Structure of online short course*

	Subject	Online configuration	Duration
Unit 1	Introductions and acclimatisation	Whole group work	1 week
Unit 2	Case studies	2 small groups	2 weeks
Unit 3	Group problem-solving	4 smaller groups	2 weeks
Unit 4	Evaluation/review	Whole group work	1 week

The online environment and training provision

The online course was delivered using the WebCT online environment. One of the main reasons for selecting this system over any other was that it was the product of choice at Sheffield University and additional technical support was available. It was also the least costly option. Within WebCT we used the chat and bulletin board tools as the focus for the online activities.

Training materials for each of these discussion tools were provided within the online environment. In addition, much of Unit 1 was given over to providing initial training sessions in the chat facility and helping participants acclimatise to the overall working environment by trying things out and asking any questions.

Tutoring

All four members of the project team were involved in tutoring the online short course during Unit 1. Thereafter there were just two tutors on the course. In recognition of the increasing trend of collaborative tutoring and provision in networked staff development we were interested to assess different models of tutoring collaboratively.

In an earlier online course delivered by the project, each of three tutors taught a different unit. The tutors were effectively working in shifts being only on duty when their unit was current. We used a different model in this staff developers' course. Here, two tutors worked on the same unit but each with a different group. In the final unit everyone, tutors included, worked together in one space. The tutors worked online throughout the course and we found that this placed greater demands on their time. However, this more continuous model of tutor participation probably results in closer working relationships with course participants due to their prolonged presence and availability.

In each of the units, the tutors were free to interpret the support needed by participants according to their own view of the demands and interests of their own online groups. They were also able to organise and provide that support according to their own schedules. Although each tutor worked with a different group online, each had a view of the other tutor's group. We found this useful as a professional development activity for tutors who were able to see alternative interpretations and responses to the tutoring task and to a similar online group. It afforded opportunities for discussion about individual and collaborative responses to various situations in the course. This visibility and sharing of practice provides flexible learning opportunities for tutors through this online form of team-teaching.

Evaluation of the online course

Evaluation of the short course was carried out within the course structure and after the course had ended. Within the course structure, Unit 4 was an opportunity for participants to work as a whole group and reflect on their experiences as well as providing a chance to consider any impact on their own practice.

When the course had finished, we sent a questionnaire to each individual participant by email. We found this electronic strategy quite effective, and sixteen of the nineteen participants completed and returned the questionnaire. The questionnaire itself was constructed with the use of Likert scales for participants to assess the value of each unit. However, the second half of the questionnaire also offered a more open format and invited participants to identify any aspects of the course they might change together with an invitation to identify the most significant/memorable moment for them in the course.

Initial findings from the evaluation

The findings below are drawn from analysis of the data from the online transcripts of Unit 4 (specifically reflecting upon the short course experience together) and also from the individual questionnaire returns sent to each participant. We have only edited the data for obvious spelling mistakes, and this is to make it more readable here.

The findings from the course evaluation form were generally very positive and this may account for the high level of questionnaire returns. On questions relating to the usability of the working environment and the tools within, participants found it easy enough to navigate around the course environment (average score of 2.92 on a scale of *1 = very easy* and *5 = very difficult*). The chat tools similarly scored an average of 2.9 on an identical scale. In terms of ease of use, participants gave an average score of 2.5 for using the bulletin board system (using the same scales).

These findings are interesting as no face-to-face training was provided. Training resources were placed online to offer documented help for using the systems and the rest was learning as we went along. The participants never met face-to-face as part of the course and most were recruited online so no prior training was given and, anyway, only 25 per cent had met the tutors as part of the regional workshops. Despite this, few difficulties were reported in using the course environment, though some of this may be attributable to the majority being online recruits and possibly therefore having more technical confidence.

The value of each unit was calculated separately, using similar Likert scales to those mentioned above, where *1 = content not useful* and *5 = very useful.* Unit 1 was to do with familiarisation with the working environment and making introductions to colleagues on the course. This unit was also about setting personal learning objectives. This unit averaged a score of 3.64.

Unit 2 divided the participants into two groups to work on a case study. The average evaluation score for this unit was 3.28. For Unit 3, where participants worked in different and smaller groups, the average score was 3.27. Unit 3 was a problem-solving task. Unit 4 was an opportunity to bring the participants back together as a whole group to discuss and reflect upon their experiences as well as to consider any implications for practice. This unit scored 3.44 and was therefore perceived as most useful.

As well as providing different models of collaborative discussion strategies with different technology combinations, the course put people in touch with each other. This social element afforded people an opportunity to discuss the current shared experience and consider it against their own local practices.

Most importantly, there was evidence that the learning from our course was already showing evidence of transfer into current networked practice:

> 'This has already fed into . . . an intra-institutional staff development course.'

> 'This has already fed into online chat sessions with students.'

The course provided contacts, resources, models and experiences that may all inform local developments. In this respect, the online course also constituted material for use in local discussions away from the course environment. There were a number of indications that participants were feeding their experiences back into their local context to develop and refine local practices:

> 'Over the last few weeks a colleague and I enrolled on two different online courses. Both courses have been running for the same time but each has had a very different structure and format. We were talking earlier about our various online experiences.'

There can be little doubt that the experience of participating as a student in an online course provides a completely different experience to that of the provider. Without such experience it is difficult to fully understand the consequences of different strategies being deployed. This was something recognised among our short course participants:

> 'My main thought is that many teachers are being required to work online but in many cases have not themselves had the experience

of working and learning in this mode. When you experience it directly, it reinforces what you have read and gives a different edge to your practice.'

Experience of networked staff development provides more than models to shape local practice. Through their experience of networked learning our staff developers began to change their attitudes towards this form of provision. This resulted in the development of a more informed perspective and a more positive view of networked strategies:

'Considering the workshop as a possible model for own practice initially looked alarmingly impossible – gradually appeared less impossible – now probable? (albeit on an unambitious scale).'

Another feature of discursive approaches to staff development is that people learn as much from each other as from providers. The providers/ tutors become facilitators of a sharing of views and previous experiences among the participants. This helps to make staff development an enjoyable and social learning experience. We also observed a number of comments (one of which is given below) made about the value of contributions made by other participants:

'Very useful, in particular through shared and recommended "resources".'

Although participants in networked staff development events may already believe that networked provision can offer them greater flexibility for participation, they sometimes fail to appreciate the attitudes of others in their workplace. Often, staff senior to themselves held conflicting attitudes to their participation or their local environment could be distracting. We found evidence that work-based learning could then become difficult.

'The competition with workplace tasks is considerable. Working online and sharing an office is hard – usually you can bury your head elsewhere if your colleagues are hyperactive but not if you need your office computer for the course.'

Some participants in networked learning also have a view of online strategies as somehow easier than traditional staff development strategies. They may believe that the flexibility means a leisurely form of partici- pation that needs little management by providers or participants. Such views were dispelled in our online course. Some of our participants recognised a need for self-discipline as something that could be appreciated only from firsthand experience. Although we found a number of participants realising this need for greater self-management rather late on in the course, this new awareness was recognised as important learning that might also transfer into aspects of practice:

'I'm certainly in future going to emphasise the need for students to plan their time very carefully when starting an online project.'

DISCUSSION

Overall the analysis of the evaluation data displays the richness of experiential approaches to networked staff development. The findings illustrate that experience of networked learning might offer:

- Changes of attitude.
- A view of different strategies deployed in different technological environments.
- A recognition that knowledge is to be gained from other participants as much as from providers.
- A developing awareness of the responsibilities of participants and providers to manage their participation.
- An opportunity to re-purpose that experience for local discussions and practices.
- A resource for discussions with others.

Networked staff development events typically last between four to six weeks and are often one-off forms of provision (Bowskill *et al.*, 2000). Among the group learning activities used in these events are online tutorials and seminars, case study discussions, role-playing and so on. These events are often delivered by a small team.

It is widely recognised that computer networks have the potential to provide resources to a mass audience and that they can be effective in offering participation to both local and remote audiences. These points are repeated only momentarily here to place the following points in context. The Internet and local networks also have implications for the delivery, structure and content of networked staff development. They have additional implications for who makes that provision as well as for whom it is made. The range of networked staff development provision, from one-off events through to the construction and maintenance of online community centres, shapes audiences quite differently, uses different tools and offers different experiences. Moreover, they place quite different responsibilities on those involved. These are points that are less well recognised.

Staff developers need to understand the networked environment and its potential for delivering teaching and learning experiences in various forms. More importantly, staff developers need to understand how this environment with its different tools and audiences may be shaped according to those different needs. They also need some knowledge of how these environments need to be managed. By way of illustration, the online events we have delivered (the online course described here being just one of several provided by the project) were very different and required quite different techniques and management by the providers.

To develop this point a little further, the dynamics of interaction and the 'behind the scenes' management issues are quite different for each online event and need to be understood more fully by those involved in networked staff development. Our online guest seminar, mentioned above, involved collaboration with the 'speaker' located in another institution. Specifically, it involved online discussions with the speaker about the content of the presentation; discussions about the nature of the involvement and participation by the speaker; the general collaborative maintenance of the working environment; and continuous collaboration during the ensuing discussions. Similarly, the course for staff developers involved liaison via email and telephone with other members of support staff as well as among the tutors involved.

Our online short course used one particular model from a range of possible models. It was delivered within a relatively closed environment; it allowed people to develop a social relationship online over an eight-week period; the participants introduced themselves to each other and worked together on different tasks; and they worked in a conferencing environment with the occasional use of real-time technologies on a diverse set of tasks. To further indicate the range of possible models, we have also presented an international guest speaker seminar (to be reported elsewhere). This was delivered to a changing, large-scale and much less knowledgeable audience over a shorter duration (three weeks), and used an email discussion list. The point here is that we can and do *shape* the environment very differently each time according to various factors and this ability is another need for potential online providers.

Networked staff development is a collaborative form of provision. The examples described by Lally and McConnell (Chapter 11, this volume) and elsewhere by Bowskill *et al.* (2000) display the cross-departmental and cross-institutional collaborations already taking place. The ability to collaborate with others online forms part of an emerging set of needs for all providers of networked teaching, learning and support. It is therefore equally important for participants in networked staff development events to have opportunities to develop such skills. Collaborative activities are therefore an important feature of networked staff development provision.

The collaborative nature of provision and the social construction of knowledge make the experience of networked group learning valuable both for academics and support staff. This is because it provides a deeper understanding, through experience and discussion, of some of the issues involved in networked group learning that helps transfer into practice elsewhere:

> 'Only now, as things close, does it feel that I'm ready to start! I have begun to realise the different kinds of approaches that one has to take online.'

This understanding arises from the current given experience being considered within the context of one's own concerns, interests, previous knowledge and any earlier experience/expectations. These individual views are tested, developed and shared through discussion with others and may give rise to common aspects of practice being developed among the group members.

The final issue we would like to mention here concerns the participation in networked staff development events and support provided in the local workplace. There are a number of issues here partly to do with self-management by participants in networked events and partly also to do with the perception and facilitation of participation by management. Academics participating in networked staff development events are a particular form of work-based learner. There is no doubt that work-based learning offers considerable flexibility and potential to extend the environment in which staff development takes place. However, the attitude of participants and their ability to schedule their involvement is key to capitalising on the flexibility of networked staff development:

> 'Time and motivation and clear goals were also important points for me. Do you think that such problems were emphasised on this course because we construed it as only half-serious to start with (somehow starting a course online without meeting face to face lessens the impact, the seriousness, of the event) but quickly learnt how serious the collaboration was once we got going and group loyalty and importance began to kick in?'

The other barrier is also the attitudes and beliefs of managers who may see this as being cost-effective or cost-reducing provision when compared alongside other forms of staff development. There is a problem of the legitimacy of participation by their staff and the perceived value of staff participating in online courses/events. More worryingly, they are often failing to make time available to staff to participate and may not always recognise any potential value in participation:

> 'In an online seminar with my PC at work my boss bursts in and wants a conversation or on my PC at home my kids burst in with some of their concerns. Even your planned time goes out the window in those circumstances.'

> 'You had to timetable yourself to look into the online class as you would a face-to-face class (feasible if you're the facilitator rather than the director). However, in practice I'm finding this impossible. For a start, managers don't see things that way – they want the two things run in parallel.'

Networked learning for supporting professional development in the workplace is an area for more research (see e.g. McConnell, 2000). The attitudes of participants and colleagues are an issue in the effectiveness of any provision. Similarly, the need to manage involvement is another issue. These issues can work against any flexibility of provision and also reduce any cost-effectiveness implied in networked staff development. This may suggest a need for an experiential programme for senior management but also a study skills programme for networked learning. Without such changes, networked staff development risks being expensive and ineffective.

REFERENCES

Alexander, W. (1999) *TALiSMAN Review of Staff Development Courses and Materials for C&IT in Teaching, Learning and Assessment.* Available from http://www.talisman.hw.ac.uk/CITreview/cit_index.html (accessed February 2004).

Beaty, L. (1995) Working Across the Hierarchy. In Brew, A. (ed.) *Directions in Staff Development.* Buckingham: SRHE and Open University Press, pp. 146–57.

Bowskill, N., Foster, J., Lally, V. and McConnell, D. (2000) Networked professional development: issues and strategies in current practice. *International Journal of Academic Development,* 5 (2), November, pp. 93–106.

Computer Based Collaborative Groupwork (CBCGW) Project (undated). Available at http://collaborate.shef.ac.uk (accessed February 2004).

Levy, P., Fowell, S.P., Bowskill, N. and Worsfold, E. (1996) NetLinkS: a national professional development project for networked learner support. *Education for Information,* 14 (4), pp. 261–78.

McConnell, D. (2000) *Implementing Computer Supported Cooperative Learning.* London: Kogan Page.

Ryan, S., Scott, B., Freeman, H. and Patel, D. (2000) *The Virtual University: The Internet and Resource-based Learning*. London: Kogan Page.

Teaching and Learning Technology Programme (undated). Available at http://www.ncteam.ac.uk/projects/tltp/index.htm (accessed February 2004).

13

Postgraduate supervisor development through ICT

Peter Kandlbinder

SUMMARY

The Postgraduate Supervisors' Development Programme at the University of Sydney has been delivered online since 1998. This chapter discusses the origins and development of a flexible learning programme for the academic development of postgraduate supervisors. This programme is supported by online materials in which academic staff are free to arrange their own progression and retrieve resources at any time that suits them and their supervisory responsibilities. It highlights the programme's participatory modes of learning which create an environment where supervisors can reflect on their own supervision as a basis for understanding their supervisory practice.

INTRODUCTION

The expectations of postgraduate students are changing as many more students consider a Ph.D. to be a professional degree rather than simply research training (Pearson, 1999). These kinds of expectations however are superimposed on already well-formulated views of what constitutes a Ph.D. It is not surprising, then, that students complain regularly that they do not receive sufficient guidance on the expectations of the candidature or that their number one complaint is communication breakdown between students and supervisors (Philips and Pugh, 1994).

When it comes to discussing their own experiences of being a Ph.D. student, postgraduate supervisors at the University of Sydney often describe feeling they had received their Ph.D. despite their supervision rather than because of it. A typical comment would be:

'I really came out of it feeling like I really did this on my own and I didn't do a very good job. I don't want it to be like that with anyone else.'

(All quotations included in this chapter are taken from interviews with thirty successful supervisors (University of Sydney, undated).)

While most successful supervisors continue to report a very good relationship with their own supervisor, even after receiving their degree, it is not uncommon to describe the experience as one of being left to fend for themselves based on the philosophy that the cream will rise to the top. Concerns are regularly expressed by current candidates that this does not always deliver a high-quality experience for postgraduate students. As time constraints increase, Ph.D.s have little alternative but to become much more structured and well defined. The misalignment between supervisors and candidates is defined as a waste of resources (Grant and Graham, 1994), which shifts the focus of improvement of supervision to tips and techniques to make the system more efficient rather than a more open, negotiated approach (Acker *et al.*, 1994).

Without a clear idea of how postgraduates learn, or the supervisor's role in the process, it is not surprising that most advice attempts to define supervision as another form of teaching. This in itself demonstrates that postgraduate supervisor pedagogy, as a distinct form of supervisor/student interaction, is not well understood. Students, coordinators and government bodies are all searching for a way to enhance the supervisory processes through a regulatory framework. Our programme for developing supervision chose to model the flexibility that assists supervisors in appreciating the unique circumstances of their students.

DEVELOPING FLEXIBLE SUPERVISORS

While there is general agreement that being a good researcher plays an important role in mentoring students into a discipline, it has been recognised for some time that this alone is not enough to become a good research supervisor (Moses, 1985). There is the personal nature to the commitment to undertake either research or supervision that gets in the way of any robust notion of pedagogy of supervisor development. With supervision taking place away from public view, where we are unlikely to be privy to these negotiations, it is little wonder that improvement of postgraduate supervision is left to advice from those who consider their own experience a success, whether directed at the supervisor (see e.g. Delamont *et al.*, 1997) or the student (see e.g. Stevens and Asmar, 1999).

The individualised, negotiated, often serendipitous nature of supervision makes it a challenge for academic development. Research supervision is a complex practice characterised by a divergence of approaches and expectations, with each candidature individually negotiated between the supervisor, candidate and department. Few other than the largest schools or departments have a formal programme of induction for supervisors new to supervision (Willcoxson, 1994).

In the absence of formal development programmes, there are three main ways of learning to supervise: (1) by being a postgraduate student, (2) through their own academic practice within a discipline, and (3) through trial and error at the interpersonal level where supervisors tread a delicate line between being supportive and critical at the same time.

As a postgraduate student, supervisors have experienced the highs and lows of supervision firsthand. In a workshop it is not unusual to hear a comment such as:

> 'My Masters supervisor was one of the most appalling supervisors I have ever come across. The only thing he wanted was publications, results and he was not interested in his students at all. My Ph.D. was completely different because I actually had my project, I designed a project and found a supervisor who actually suited that project.'

What, in general, made these experiences poor is what one supervisor calls 'the deep-end principle':

> 'My own Ph.D. supervisor had total trust and faith in me, to a worrying point, where he believed things I was doing were right when I didn't believe they were right. So I was very much on my own. I wouldn't subject any of my students to that.'

These perceptions of poor supervision tend to describe supervisors who were not reflective of their own experiences. An attitude one coordinator at the University of Sydney has come up against is:

> 'Well, I had to go through that, why shouldn't they?'

These are supervisors who have formed the belief that preparation of a research thesis is a trial by fire and candidates have to be seen to struggle, otherwise their work cannot be original or at the cutting edge.

Reflection is equally critical for supervisors who have had positive experiences:

'I think I had a very good supervisor. I don't think I mirrored his particular style, but . . . I think having a good role model at the time I was learning to supervise actually helped me.'

Without good models of practice, it is not surprising that most supervisors have been influenced by their own experiences, even if this simply provides a foil to oppose.

ONLINE ACADEMIC DEVELOPMENT

With over 3000 graduate students at the Doctoral and Masters level, the University of Sydney is one of the leading research-orientated universities in Australia. The challenge for supervisor development in this environment is that supervisors come to academic development programmes with differing experiences, contexts and disciplinary expectations but are unable to see models of good practice. The University of Sydney Institute for Teaching and Learning meets this challenge by providing a range of resources to encourage supervisors to reflect on the consequences of supervisory practices through the Postgraduate Supervisors' Development Programme. This is a long-running and successful programme that was originally offered as a series of workshops aimed particularly at those who are new to supervision. Originally developed with seed funding made available by the Pro-Vice-Chancellor (Research), the programme moved to its new format when it faced the realities of limited funding which made an extensive programme of workshops unsustainable.

Interviews with successful supervisors clearly demonstrate that it is the supervisors' own supervision and reflecting on these experiences that has the greatest impact on what they do with their students. Simply understanding how successful supervisors learned to be effective has played a crucial role in designing a programme for the development of supervisors. With successful supervisors stressing the interpersonal relationship, co-learning and encouragement, it quickly became apparent that there is a need to be more than a repository of information on the University's regulations and policies. But neither could it focus simply on developing techniques and methods for effective supervision. The determining principle of the programme has been to demonstrate the diversity in supervisory practice, and to support supervisors in reflecting on how they compare to their own experiences of postgraduate supervision.

The multifaceted picture that emerged on the role of a supervisor provided the primary guidance in the appropriate process for postgraduate supervisor development. A supervisor is invariably described as a mentor, a facilitator and manager, guiding students to become independent researchers in their chosen field. Improvement of supervisory practice requires a programme that supports each of these roles. The programme also recognises that successful supervisors additionally have to keep up with disciplinary knowledge to be able to effectively mentor students into the discipline, but along with that they have a role in providing a structured environment and managing that process.

A survey of University of Sydney supervisors suggested the biggest barrier to participation in academic development was lack of time. The majority of supervisors unwittingly accept their first instance of supervisory responsibility rather than consciously choosing to supervise. It is not uncommon to be asked to co-supervise a student to provide an area of specialist expertise and to then find one taking over the responsibility for another supervisor's student. The almost accidental nature of starting to supervise means that most learn on the job. Often the busiest academics are also those with the most postgraduate students. With the increasing pressures on academic life today, supervisors are unable to prioritise academic development ahead of other responsibilities. Any postgraduate supervisor's development programme needs to be as flexible as possible at all levels to remove the barriers to participation perceived about the face-to-face workshop format.

Shifting to flexible delivery has been an evolutionary progression best described as a move from information sharing towards enquiry into postgraduate supervision. Each stage in this development may be seen as a focus on an increasingly more complex dimension of postgraduate supervision. The first phase involved information collection and dissemination, providing an easy access point to the University's regulations, policies and codes of practice. The second phase developed learning materials with activities to make sense of existing information on postgraduate supervision and to encourage reflection on practice.

The guiding principle of the current phase is to turn the obvious research abilities of supervisors towards researching their own practice. As the Faculties most represented in the programme are the health sciences, medicine and science, many participants have extensive experience in discipline-based research but limited experience in researching educational practices. While activity based, these modules were further enhanced with supporting online discussions and supervisor case studies. A problem-based approach to the Postgraduate Supervisors' Development Programme is an attempt to develop an educational solution from a process of systematic analysis that identifies the problem being solved, locates it within a broader research framework and applies a contextually appropriate educational solution.

POSTGRADUATE SUPERVISORS' DEVELOPMENT PROGRAMME

The Postgraduate Supervisors' Development Programme is an innovative flexible learning programme supported with materials delivered via the Web (University of Sydney, undated). The programme represents an innovative approach to postgraduate supervision development in that it provides the opportunity to study where and when it suits the supervisor. The flexible learning programme aims to assist participants make sense of postgraduate supervision using a framework that models the learning processes of postgraduate students. In an effort to guide a more rigorous reflection of improving supervisory practice, a new learning environment has been developed to permit academic staff to set their own learning goals and arrange their own level of participation in the programme. Supervisors are asked to reflect on their journey to becoming a supervisor, drawing first on their own experiences of being supervised. The process is broken into four separate but related forms of enquiry starting with the descriptive research, followed by a validation in theory, which leads to describing the general principles of their supervision. In the final stage these principles are returned to their specific settings, students and tasks.

Guided by trigger questions, supervisors are encouraged to systematically construct (and reconstruct) their individual conceptual network of strategies and theories of supervision. The case studies of successful supervision enable participants to reflect on their supervisory practice, clarify their understanding of what constitutes effective supervision in their context, and share their insights and experience with colleagues from within and across disciplines.

The key feature of the programme is its multi-layered design that emphasises collaboration within the entire university community. It is somewhat unique as an academic development programme in that it includes the involvement of senior academics of the university and postgraduate coordinators who contribute their time and resources to the programme. A challenge has been to maintain a balance between the strong commitment to the use of the experiences of the participants as the basis for reflection on supervision and to individualise the materials to meet the participant's particular background and interests. The programme is sustained through these different levels of interaction that equally engage novice supervisors and highly successful experienced supervisors alike.

The overall design of the programme is an integration of information on the regulatory requirements, practice and group activities. This provides a range of experiences that identify the key skills of successful supervisors and creates opportunities to transfer their application into practice. The programme is structured around a combination of the postgraduate supervisor's website, face-to-face workshops, and peer discussion and review. There are three corresponding activity areas in the programme: web-based resources, independent study modules and group-based activities.

WORLD WIDE WEB-BASED RESOURCES

As a flexible learning programme an overarching goal has been to provide access to learning resources in a mode which permits participation at any time that suits time-constrained members of academic staff. Academics need to be able to engage with the programme in a timely manner according to their level of need, which may vary from the most straightforward contact details to the more complex, ethical questions regularly faced by supervisors, such as the ownership of intellectual property. The website reinforces the three levels of postgraduate supervision support identified in the programme. Consequently, there is a choice of three ways to access the online resources: by browsing through available material, enrolling to complete independent study modules, or participating in online discussions. In this way the participants make the choice about whether they simply need information on postgraduate supervision or access to skills development through structured learning experiences, or to contribute to a network of like-minded supervisors.

Resource material on postgraduate supervision

The browsing section of the website is open to anyone interested in postgraduate supervision. It is a source of links to reference material on postgraduate supervision, including the University of Sydney regulations, policies, the *Postgraduate Supervisors Handbook,* and links to appropriate committees and associations, such as the Sydney University Postgraduate Student's Association (SUPRA). It contains bibliographic references, links to government reports, case studies submitted by successful supervisors plus handouts and issue papers from the workshops.

The purpose of these resources is to demonstrate the institutional expectations and standards of successful supervision. It attempts to represent the diversity in the university culture of postgraduate research supervision. In so doing it maintains participation of high-ranking, experienced and successful supervisors of the University such as the workshop presenters who provide resources they consider relevant to the new supervisors.

INDEPENDENT STUDY MODULES

There are six independent study modules, each taking at least an hour of study time. The modules are designed for supervisors who would like to work through the resource material in a more formalised course of study. They present a process by which the standards and expectations demonstrated by successful supervisors may be met. Case studies of successful supervision are integrated into the self-study material and are also made available in the resources section of the website. Supervisors who would like their participation in the programme formally assessed do so by developing their own case study, which is made available through the resources section.

The independent study modules present a series of self-assessment activities on key issues of postgraduate supervision. They are organised around six stages of supervision: getting started, first meeting, managing the process, the end of year review, writing, and finishing. Each stage is framed by trigger material with activities to assist supervisors to understand fully the issues relevant to this stage of postgraduate supervision. Exploration of the questions raised by the trigger material is supported by other elements of the programme (web-based resources, face-to-face workshops and peer discussion).

Working through the activities provides the foundation for participants to document their supervisory practice. This then contributes to the reference section as case study material. Although designed as a coherent programme, modules may be accessed individually to address a particular need. The most frequently accessed modules focus on preparing for the end-of-year review followed by preparing for supervision.

Participants in the programme reported that engaging with the material in the modules assisted them to gain a better understanding of the constitution of Masters and Ph.D. programmes. It also helped to define the student–supervisor relationship and cement ideas about the importance of good communication. The modules additionally assisted some supervisors in developing a research culture among students. In one case, this was so successful that the faculty involved decided to further support the development of postgraduate research skills through the appointment of a sub-dean.

Participants' learning goals

The programme is password protected and requires formal registration to receive access to the modules. By registering in the programme, supervisors signal a commitment to study postgraduate supervision. Registration provides an opportunity for participants to set their own learning goals. It also permits the programme coordinator to identify participants' specific needs and negotiate with them their level of involvement, target the resource materials to their interests and provide support to individual supervisors by addressing their questions and concerns. Registered participants are automatically notified of work-shops, contact details of other registered participants, reports from support group activities and material provided by guest presenters.

Registration involves a brief questionnaire in which supervisors indicate their interest in postgraduate supervision and participants are asked to nominate a date when they would like to be removed from the registration list. The learning goals submitted by the supervisors have a two-pronged role. They provide the ITL with a record of the important issues currently facing supervisors. Moreover, it is an opportunity for supervisors on the area they need to engage with in the programme, in a replication of the fine-tuning of research questions. To date supervisors have indicated a wide range of learning goals. These include:

- Giving advice in planning and structuring research material.
- Establishing what is required of both the student/supervisor in terms of interaction and goals.
- Motivating discouraged students.
- Stimulating candidates to publish research.
- Understanding the administrative requirements of the various stages of the Ph.D.
- Encouraging students to think critically.
- Finding the line between guiding and instructing.
- Assessment and development of candidates' competencies to complete projects.
- Provision of constructive feedback.
- Policies at departmental level for supervisory practice.

GROUP-BASED ACTIVITIES

A difficulty created by the implicit nature of postgraduate supervision practices is the uncertainty of the reasons some practices work and this makes it difficult to transfer them to other supervisors, other problems or other social settings. While supervisors have traditionally used their personal experiences developed through insight and trial and error to build the craft of their personal knowledge that is useful in their own particular area, a lack of reflection, as was suggested above, allows supervisors to hear what they expect to hear (research is hard), rather than what is actually being said (I need some help).

With the awareness that learning is both situated and progressively developed through activity (Wenger, 1998), group learning becomes the mechanism for promoting a deeper understanding of the supervisor's own approaches to postgraduate supervision through collaborating on complex problems. The programme provides two opportunities for supervisors to have their assumptions challenged in light of their decision-making as a key to refining their personal knowledge.

The first of these is the online discussion forum wherein the website supports peer interaction so that supervisors may discuss issues of postgraduate supervision. An email list of all registered participants is maintained for administrative purposes, such as announcing updates to the website and publicising events such as workshops. Workshop presenters' notes are also made available through a posting in the forum. There are structured discussions facilitated by a moderator discussing his or her own contribution in the form of a short paper or the implications of some wider issue in the academic research community. Participants are also invited to contribute their responses to wider issues in the higher education sector to do with postgraduate supervision which are collected and included with the resources materials.

The discussion forum runs independently but parallel to the independent study materials and maintains the cross-disciplinary nature of the programme. It is in this forum that the results of the independent study activities may be posted or general issues of interest discussed. While the initial design anticipated that there would be a need for a collegial environment to discuss issues of postgraduate supervision, when surveyed on their use of the online forum, participants were more likely to report informal and naturally forming peer support groups formed as the consequence of participating in the programme. It was found that after sharing ideas on the online discussion, supervisors tended to telephone colleagues identified online and arrange to meet informally to talk over issues.

WORKSHOPS

As a programme of study the PGSDP has always been conceived of as more than just placing information about workshops and their hand-outs on a website. By the same token, the feedback from earlier workshops indicated that meeting face-to-face still fulfilled a need, with the participants describing workshops as overwhelmingly 'worthwhile' and 'worthy of support'. Attendance was intermittent mainly due to the large time commitment of the workshops.

Each year the programme schedules two face-to-face workshops during the non-teaching time in each semester. Workshops provide an alternative mechanism for supervisors who prefer to come together to discuss post-graduate supervision. The workshops are opportunities for participants to hear examples of successful supervision, discuss issues related to their own practice and to work through case study material. It is also a chance to cross faculty and departmental boundaries to explore the context of supervision and its relation to all other academic responsibilities. Comparing the humanities and science-based case histories, for example, always fuels a lively discussion of the purpose behind a research thesis.

The themes of the workshops reflect the two major strategies for learning to supervise identified by experienced supervisors. One workshop focuses on the roles and responsibilities of supervisors. It provides training in skills for small group learning in preparation for the establishment of peer support groups. The other workshop focuses on the interpersonal skills required to structure and manage the supervision process. Activities to practise key skills include communicating with students, dealing with problems and providing meaningful feedback. In addition, it is an opportunity to take stock of the programme and the participants' learning goals. Both workshops provide information, case studies of effective supervision and opportunities to practise these skills so that participants may take away ideas and examples of strategies to implement in their own practice.

For the ITL, workshops help develop a profile for quality supervision within the University and are an invaluable source of informal feedback from workshop participants. It also allows supervisors to gauge their own approach, relative to the wider university community. Participants in the workshops invariably ask for more opportunities for group discussion, particularly after hearing case histories of successful supervision from experienced supervisors. They enjoy exploring a range of supervisory situations and expectations of supervisors. By hearing from successful supervisors and being able to discuss problems and strategies, the workshops showcase the firsthand observations of experienced supervisors as well as modelling effective supervision.

FUTURE CHALLENGES FOR THE PROGRAMME

Feedback from participants, coordinators and senior academics of the University indicates that the programme continues the good work begun by the earlier workshops, with the added flexibility of modules which 'allows thinking about the principles of postgraduate supervision outside the workshop format'. The multiple points at which the programme is now entered, plus the data which indicate that the programme is reaching a substantially broader cross-section of academic staff, justify the shift to a flexibly delivered programme.

Participants in the programme have reported adopting strategies in their practice such as seeing students more regularly, offering clearer documentation of meetings with students, and listening more carefully to what students are saying. The independent study materials and online resources (discussion and resource section) provide a range of learning tools that are reportedly migrating into supervisory practice. Many are now aware of the importance of introducing new students to post-graduate networks and consider the development of mentorship schemes between new and experienced candidates. This indicates that participants in the Postgraduate Supervisor Development Programme are looking at issues of the structure of the supervisory relationship, which is a positive outcome in light of the aims of the programme.

For a sustained improvement in supervision practice the strong record of supervisor support of many of the University's schools and departments needs be implemented across the University as a whole. Postgraduate coordinators play the key role in providing support for the development of postgraduate supervisors at a local level, while some coordinators acknowledged that there was an increased intensity in the department related to the importance of supervisory responsibilities. This intensity was due partly to students becoming more assertive in understanding what was expected in the relationship. Support groups continue to be set up in a number of departments.

All coordinators commented that they had been receiving publicity regularly (emails and print publicity) from the ITL in relation to workshops. A few coordinators were not aware that part of the pro-gramme was being delivered online through web-based modules. One coordinator encouraged two staff members of the department to attend and then facilitate an academic development morning on supervision. In this instance, staff who attended the workshop encouraged others to access the web-based materials.

Perhaps the greatest challenge for the future of the programme will be to overcome the time pressures so often mentioned as a limiting factor in staff accessing the programme and putting these principles into practice. Feedback from participants has pointed to the need for more structure in online discussions to ensure higher levels of participa-tion. Continued collaboration with the postgraduate coordinators and rewarding supervisors' participation in the programme are two important strategies for the programme as it moves into its next stage of development.

CONCLUSION

The Postgraduate Supervisors' Development Programme has demonstrated that it is possible to use online academic development as a means to provide new and experienced supervisors with an opportunity to engage in discussion and reflection relating to postgraduate supervision. A steady increase in the number of supervisors registered to complete the programme demonstrates that the combination of the workshop programme and web-based resources continues to meet the diverse needs of postgraduate supervisors at the University of Sydney. The web-based resources allowed supervisors to complete the programme in their own time while addressing their immediate learning goals. Workshops provide the important opportunity to interact with supervisors from other schools and departments, and to share experiences of successful supervision. This is an endorsement for the individualised, negotiated, sometime serendipitous curricular structure that tries to capture the tenor of the nature of supervision by providing supervisors with the maximum choice, and that also acknowledges their status within their disciplines, while doing so in the context which meets the regulatory responsibilities the University has set for quality supervision of its students.

ACKNOWLEDGEMENT

The author would like to acknowledge the work of Tai Peseta for her work in developing the successful supervisor case studies, supporting the programme and collecting all the evaluative data.

REFERENCES

Acker, S., Hill, T. and Black, E. (1994) Thesis supervision in the social sciences: managed or negotiated? *Higher Education*, 28, pp. 483–98.

Delamont, S., Atkinson, P. and Parry, O. (1997) *Supervising the PhD: A Guide to Success*. Buckingham: The Society for Research into Higher Education and Open University Press.

Grant, B. and Graham, A. (1994) Guidelines for discussion: a tool for managing postgraduate education. In Zuber-Skerritt, O. and Ryan, Y. (eds) *Quality in Postgraduate Education*. London: Kogan Page.

Moses, I. (1985) *Supervising Postgraduates*. Campbelltown: HERDSA.

Pearson, M. (1999) The changing environment for doctoral education in Australia: implications for quality management, improvement and innovation. *Higher Education Research and Development*, 18 (3), pp. 268–87.

Phillips, E. and Pugh, D. (1994) *How to get a PhD*. Buckingham: Open University Press.

Stevens, K. and Asmar, C. (1999) *Doing Postgraduate Research in Australia.* Melbourne: Melbourne University Press.

University of Sydney (undated) *In Supervisors' Words: An Insider's View of Postgraduate Supervision.* Available at http://www.itl.usyd.edu.au/ctl/ (accessed February 2004).

Wenger, E. (1998) *Communities of Learning.* Cambridge: Cambridge University Press.

Willcoxson, L. (1994) Postgraduate supervision practices: strategies for development and change. *Higher Education Research and Development,* 13 (2), pp. 157–66.

14

Cutting out computer anxiety

(A scissors-and-cardboard approach to learning about computers)

Vic Tandy and Glynis Cousin

SUMMARY

This chapter describes the innovative teaching of computer technology through the de/construction of cardboard computers. The teaching and learning activities and outcomes in relation to this innovation will be presented together with a discussion of their bearing on the creation of an effective learning environment. The chapter concludes by drawing out the transferable features of this study particularly with regard to 'computer-anxious' students.

THE TEACHING AND LEARNING PROBLEM: IMPEDANCE MISMATCH

This study relates to a group of humanities students who opt to take an information technology module which requires that they learn how to provide a fully costed project proposal document to include a specification for computer hardware. In the first two years of this module's life, only 20 per cent of students managed to offer a satisfactory specification. While the lecturer worked hard to transmit key information to the students and the students evidently strained to understand the lecturer, there was a problem, to use an electrical engineering concept, of 'impedance mismatch'; namely, a loss of energy from one circuit (the lecturer's input) to another (student receptivity). In the light of this mismatch, the need for a rethink about how to teach this part of the module was pressing. Clearly, an instructional style that had worked for more technically minded students at the University was not working for this group of humanities students (both male and female). In the first instance, an issue of learning style was observed.

HOLISTIC AND SERIALIST LEARNERS

The differences we observed between the technically inclined students and those from the humanities seemed to fit the differences between holistic and serialist learners (Pask, 1975). Whereas the technically inclined tended to be comfortable with the presentation of information in a sequential fashion, the humanities students appeared to need a more holistic approach. As with any learning style typology, there is a danger of overdrawing this difference, not least because the technically inclined student will have the advantage of more relevant cultural capital with which to learn from a step-by-step approach. However, by thinking about the respective learning needs of students as roughly falling into these categories, it was possible to review the teaching methods around the need to present the parts via the whole rather than vice versa.

The learning style perspective also fits with the gestalt approach to learning which insists that learners need to be presented with the big picture in order to make sense of its detail, since the whole is always more than the sum of its parts. This premise is problematic for IT teaching because so much of it is about procedural, incrementally gained knowledge which does not lend itself to an obvious holistic approach. In computer technology, the big picture is the fully assembled machine, but getting students to dismantle a new functional computer was clearly too risky and costly an option. In drawing on his experience of using cardboard models to help clients to visualise devices in design engineering, Tandy formulated the idea of getting students to construct a rudimentary model of a computer from cardboard. In this way, it was hoped that the students would experience and quite literally *feel* the problems they needed to solve. As a leading theorist of experiential learning, Rogers (in Rogers and Freiberg, 1994) insists that the more personally involved students are in the tasks set, the more they will internalise what they need to learn. Arguably, this makes particularly good sense where students are anxious about the subject in hand; it also makes good sense to allow students to come to know something of their subject through the sense of touch. The tactile, as psychologists will tell us, gives human beings their first means by which to understand.

ENGAGING THE TACTILE

The Italian educationalist Montessori (Hainstock, 1997) was among the first educationalists to point out that an important early phase of learning proceeds through touch. With this in mind, Montessori recommended that before children are formally taught the alphabet, they be given bricks with each letter etched in relief so that children could feel how 'A', 'B' and so on felt to the touch before grappling with its meaning. This phase of tactile familiarity enabled the child to befriend the objects of later formal learning and thus to be less anxious about them; it also enabled some early cognitive activity around the meaning of these letters, though it did not strain children to formalise this before they were ready to do so. In today's jargon, this was neck-down teaching (Claxton, 1997) because it was about getting a feel for the subject – in our case quite literally, as one student acknowledged, *'it was very helpful to have a "hands-on" approach that is different from just being told about it'.*

The equivalent of Montessori's bricks was a photocopied state-of-the-art motherboard and components represented in outline with no specification. Students were required to explore contemporary computer magazines to find the latest specification and cost of the components of computers. Different groups of students were given a description of the range and functions of a computer. Some students had to create the cheapest computer capable of word processing while others were given a budget for a high-end multimedia machine. Students cut out cardboard representations of the various hardware components, noting necessary details on them before sticking these on the appropriate place on the motherboard. Each phase of construction was preceded by a whole group discussion about the function and scope of a particular component and the relevant needs of each group's specification.

This construction process spanned three two-hour sessions spaced over three weeks, and the following notes from the lecturer (Tandy) illustrate the kind of dynamic this teaching intervention produced:

> One student used his virtual funds to specify a very fast Intel CPU with 4Mb of RAM. This was discussed among the group and another student pointed out that her book said Windows 98 needed at least 16Mb of RAM. In fact, any performance gain from the fast CPU would be lost by the choice of memory (it probably would not work at all). Along with the rest of the group, I proposed possible alternatives. Finally, the student decided to reduce the specification of the processor and use 32Mb of RAM, which would be better for the purpose specified. Physically pulling out the cardboard chip and replacing the cardboard RAM helped fix this process firmly in the student's mind.
>
> Interestingly, another student designed his own ZIP drive and added it to his cardboard computer.

3-D NOTE-TAKING

Feedback from two cohorts of students confirmed our observations that our pedagogy of ' feeling and doing' was working. We particularly liked the image of '3-D note-taking' offered by one student:

'I found that constructing a computer out of cardboard was a very effective way of learning. It was like taking notes in 3-D.'

Further student comments add to this sense of 'vivid' learning:

'The construction of cardboard computers is such a stroke of genius that I don't think there could possibly be a better way to teach students about computer hardware.'

'"Making" a computer was a really good idea. Much better than just sitting making notes.'

'Using a visual aid is far more useful than simply having lectures.'

'It is more active involvement. You can see for yourself, rather than just be told about it.'

'In my opinion, the construction of cardboard computers is an excellent way for students who have little knowledge of computers to learn about computer hardware.'

We were particularly interested in the feedback from the following students because they specifically defined themselves as 'nervous' or 'anxious' about handling computers:

'It was better to actually be able to build something and learn at the same time, rather than just sitting and listening – it was much more interesting.'

'It was useful to learn about each part of the computer as we went along.'

'The visual explanation made things much easier to understand.'

Taken as a whole, the above comments suggest that although changes were introduced to address failing students, our framework proved to be a better one for any kind of student. As is often the case in education, fixing a problem for 'weaker' students often generates good teaching practice at a more general level. It is also the case that reviewing the teaching and learning activities invariably requires a review of forms of assessment.

ASSSESSMENT MATTERS

Biggs (1999) argues that building an effective learning environment requires an alignment of important elements in curriculum design, teaching method, learner orientation and the form of assessment used. There is not much explicitly in Biggs about how affective issues such as learner anxiety are brought into this design, though his insistence on a constructivist understanding of the learner implicitly embraces this question. According to the constructivist perspective, learners' biographies (both as students and more generally) will interact with what they must learn and teachers must be sensitive to this. Biggs offers a concept of 'constructive alignment' to explain a process by which the teaching, curriculum design and assessment 'out there' can be made to fit with the learners' world 'in here'. In applying this concept to our context, it was clearly important to make adjustments to the assessment mode, not least to take account of the 'computer-anxious' among the student group. If learners are nervous, they will be all the more so if exams are stacked at the end of a difficult learning experience. In short, there is no point in offering more interesting and effective ways of learning if the assessment remains daunting.

Thomas and Bain's (1984) work has shown that when teaching interventions and learning strategies are ineffective, inappropriate assessment will often be part of the problem. The assessment on this module, following an instructional style of teaching, was based on a final written test (the production of a specification). This model of teaching and assessment was clearly a very poor encouragement to 'deep learning' (Marton and Saljo, 1976) because it invited an investment of effort (probably anxious effort) into the last-minute revision of 'facts' abstracted from their usefulness. The actual method of assessment was fixed because the specification formed part of the overall assessment, which was to produce a (fictitious) bid for funds within guidelines borrowed from BT's University Development Awards.

However, changing the mode of teaching removed the gulf between the teaching and assessment. It became more of a continuum and closer to the kind of constructive alignment that Biggs (1999) advises. As in the original methodology the students were aware of the specification they would need to produce, but the two stages of 'instruction' and 'do' became one problem-solving exercise. Students not only learned about the hardware but also about how to decide what hardware was appropriate for their needs. The cardboard computer construction required all parts to be assembled and thus it was not possible for students to dodge learning about some of these parts. Students were still expected to come up with an individual specification for the project but it became a less awesome prospect because they had rehearsed how to do this within a group. As a result of these changes, the number of students able to present a satisfactory specification rose to 80 per cent. All the students, even those self-defined as nervous, reported an increased understanding of computers. What follows is a selection of student comments to illustrate:

'I understand about the internal works of computers now.'

'By knowing what's going on inside you can understand why the computers always take forever.'

'I now know what is being talked about in TV adverts.'

'I now know what a processor and what RAM is.'

'I now understand the basic terms and know roughly how things work.'

Although we were encouraged by these comments and by the formal performance of the students, one student who described himself as a 'nervous' learner of computers offered the apparently contradictory statement:

'I have learnt more but I don't think my confidence has increased.'

This comment points to the complexity of computer anxiety and reminds us that its defeat is no easy matter. We turn finally to a general discussion of this issue.

COMPUTER ANXIETY

Townsend *et al.*'s (1998) examination of self-concept and anxiety among students studying social science statistics showed that you can get better at something without *feeling* better about it. Clearly this was the case with our last quoted student, and though we had succeeded in raising his performance, we did not manage to increase his confidence. In an extensive study of 'technophobia', Brosnan (1998) has indicated that being at home with computers is a matter of identity as much as a matter of skill acquisition. Ability in a subject is not a predictor of confidence because what learners think about their ability does not always coincide with their real ability. Studies in gender and subject comfort engage with this issue a great deal (see e.g. Brosnan, 1998; Grundy, 1996; Shaw, 1995) because what we think we are good at is often tied up with our gendered identity. In our study, we noted the humanities/science divide of students and the learner styles along that divide, though, of course, as Shaw (1995) has argued, this divide interacts with a history of gendered baggage.

This history has meant that students (regardless of their sex) who choose humanities often do so against science and technical subjects rather than *instead* of them and vice versa. Such choices involve identity decisions about where abilities, strengths and weaknesses lie. The computer-anxious are often anxious because they do not believe themselves to be 'good at' computers and this belief can result in a self-fulfilling prophecy. Although his concern is with language learning, Krashen's concept of an 'affective filter hypothesis' is relevant to our discussion, not least because computer skill acquisition is itself a form of language learning. Krashen (1995) argues that anxiety acts as a filter that comes between the learner and the language he or she must grasp (enthusiasm and confidence will work in the opposite direction of course). In Krashen's view, this problem is addressed by paying due attention to the 'comprehensible input' a teacher offers the learner. For Krashen, cognitive ability is inextricably tied up with personal safety issues and, for this reason, teachers have to think about what is emotionally manageable for their students.

We believe that demystifying the workings of the computer in the ways we have described has helped students to gain access to the language of computers in non-threatening ways. We also believe that the methods we introduced to our students are transferable to learners of computer skills at a broader level.

OPEN THE BOX!

Although students learning IT skills do not need to have the kind of detailed specification knowledge taught in the module we have described, it may be worth de/constructing computers for the 'computer-anxious' in order to break down some of the mystery, as the following student suggests:

'Seeing the inside of a computer removed a lot of the mystery 'cos computers are just a box, with no indication of what is inside.'

One of the difficulties with IT training is that it rests on the acquisition of procedural knowledge. This acquisition is largely a matter of memorisation allied to the psychomotor functions related to simple technical functions (e.g. switching on, use of mouse). On the face of it, this should mean that learning is simply acquired because it reduces to the task of remembering. Yet we also know that anxiety gets in the way of remembering as Krashen (1995) has argued. Opening the box may help to reduce learner stress just as a basic introduction to the inner workings of the flight deck is known to help those with flying phobias. In particular, exposing how a computer works through de/construction may bring hesitant learners more closely to the heart of the subject. Feeling unsafe about a skill or subject to be grasped means feeling too much distance from it. As Shaw (1995) suggests, when learners declare themselves to be 'no good at' a subject, they feel a lack of intimacy, whereas:

'Feeling "at home" in a subject, being able to "get into it" and use its conventions for one's own expressive purposes is akin to using a teddy bear, blanket or whatever as a tool for mental growth.'

Dismantling a computer for learners who need to acquire only basic computer skills may seem to be a circuitous route towards skill acquisition, but if it helps them to feel more 'at home' with the subject, it will be a journey worth making. We are currently researching the effectiveness of such a journey for students wishing to increase their confidence with online learning.

CONCLUSION

In describing innovative teaching interventions for very specific purposes, we hope that we have drawn out a number of ideas and issues of interest to those teaching ICT to any kind of student (or pupil). In particular, we hope that we have shown that the experiential model of learning we have established provides a novel and effective way of introducing computers to what might otherwise be groups of resistant learners.

REFERENCES

Biggs, J. (1999) *Teaching for Quality Learning at University*, Buckingham: SRHE/OUP.

Brosnan, M. (1998) *Technophobia – The Psychological Impact of Information Technology*, London: Routledge.

Claxton, G. (1997) *Hare Brain, Tortoise Mind*, London: Fourth Estate.

Grundy, F. (1996) *Women and Computers*, Exeter, Intellect Books.

Hainstock, E.G. (1997) *The Essential Montessori: An Introduction to the Woman, the Writings, the Mind*, New York: Plume.

Krashen, S. (1995) *Principles and Practice in Second Language Acquisition*, Harmondsworth: Penguin.

Marton, F. and Saljo, R. (1976) On qualitative differences in learning: outcome and process. *British Journal of Educational Psychology*, 46, pp. 4–11.

Pask, G. (1975) *Conversation, Cognition and Learning*, New York: Elsevier.

Rogers, C. and Freiberg, J. (1994) *Freedom to Learn*, Columbus, OH: Merrill.

Shaw, J. (1995) *Education, Gender and Anxiety*, London, Taylor & Francis.

Thomas, P.R. and Bain, J.D. (1984) Contextual dependence of learning approaches: the effects of assessments. *Human Learning*, 3, pp. 227–40.

Townsend, M., Moore, D.W., Tuck, B.F. and Wilton, K.M. (1998) University students studying social studies statistics within a cooperative learning structure. *Educational Psychology*, 18(1), pp. 41–54.

15

Dealing with Internet cheating: countering the online 'paper mills'

Margaret Fain and Peggy Bates

SUMMARY

The Internet is changing the way students cheat. The quick availability of so much 'free' information and the quickness of 'cut and paste' has created a generation of students who often seem more at ease moving information around than comprehending it. A chance remark by a mathematics professor to the authors some years ago led to the development of a staff 'teaching effectiveness' workshop at Coastal Carolina University entitled *Cheating: Paper Mills and You* (Fain and Bates, 1999, updated 2003). The workshop was designed to introduce teaching staff to the issue of Internet-based plagiarism, the current state of Internet 'paper mills', detection and tracking down of plagiarised papers, and solutions to combating Internet plagiarism. This chapter expands on that original presentation to provide guidance to teaching staff, librarians and administrative staff who are grappling with the issues of plagiarism in a wired environment. The innocent question that the naive professor had asked was: 'Is it true that students can get research papers off the Internet?'

INTRODUCTION

Cheating in colleges and universities has been going on since the beginning of organised education. Passing off another student's paper as their own is a time-honoured tradition among students pressed for time or uninterested in the topic. For some time in the United States, 'paper mills' have advertised in campus newspapers or in the back of magazines that were popular with college students. For a small fee, these services would mail the student a pre-written paper. Due to the time factor and cost, relatively few students took advantage of the services. With the advent of the Internet, this has changed. Paper mills can now supply papers that may be downloaded instantaneously, cutting turn-around time and costs. Their prime customers have been some of the biggest users of the Internet and word of mouth spread the news. Just type 'research papers' in any Internet search engine to find a long list of Internet paper providers, and not only local ones. The global community of the Internet means that papers may be found in all languages and from a variety of international sources. No longer relegated to the back alleys of college campuses, the term 'paper industry' is flourishing, prosperous, and reaching a much larger and younger audience.

CURRENT STATE OF CHEATING

For many students, lofty ideas about honesty and integrity have very little to do with the 'real world' or why they are going to college. Many have no idea what an 'education' really is; they have come to college to get a credential that will allow them to pursue a chosen career. The acquisition of this credential is more important than the way it is acquired. Some students view any course not directly related to their major subject as a waste of time. Other students will cheat or plagiarise to maintain high grade point averages (GPAs), experiencing tremendous pressure from their parents, graduate schools, corporate recruiters or themselves to get good grades. Some students manage to make it to college thinking anything and everything on the Internet is public domain. They simply do not know what constitutes plagiarism, as their secondary school teachers did not cover the topic. Others think it is no longer 'socially un-acceptable' to cheat to get ahead; they cheat in self-defence, since other students in their classes are cheating already which creates unfair competition. Students may feel that their teachers don't really read their papers, so why bother to do the work. Others use the Internet as a last hope, when they have run out of time and energy to create the original work expected of them at university.

RELUCTANCE TO REPORT PLAGIARISM

Another part of the problem is the university teacher's reluctance to report plagiarism to university authorities when it occurs. This reluctance is seen in the preference for handling suspected plagiarism privately between the teacher and student, as a counselling matter or not at all.

The stigma of plagiarism inhibits teachers from discussing the issue with their peers. Without knowing the scope of the problem, teachers believe that plagiarism in their class is a direct reflection of their teaching ability, not part of a broader problem. Some feel that they are in the business of teaching specific subject matter, not discipline or moral values.

An additional matter (but one which also inhibits formal reporting) is determined by many institutions' rules and procedures which require the implementation of an almost court of law set of procedures before meaningful action may be taken against the plagiarist – these rules tend to focus on local warnings rather than formal institution-wide action.

Knowledge of copyright issues and the ability to cite sources correctly should come into the class with the student, and does not need to be taught again. Circumstances in universities today (with administrations pushing student retention, litigious students, students threatening physical harm) are not conducive to 'going out on a limb' to prosecute plagiarism. Then there is always the fear of 'sticking your neck out' to prosecute and having the administration or trustees not only dismiss your allegations of plagiarism as insignificant, but damaging your career in the process.

PLAGIARISM EDUCATION

In order to understand the scope of the issue, university Faculty and administrators should take the time to become cognisant of the various issues involved. There are several excellent websites maintained by colleagues worldwide that discuss plagiarism and provide guidance for dealing with the problem. These sites are aimed primarily at university teachers and provide guidance in plagiarism prevention. They cover everything from designing and guiding research papers to methods for educating students about the pitfalls of plagiarism. Well-established examples include:

- *Anti-Plagiarism Strategies for Research Papers* (Harris, 2002).
- *Instructors Guide to Internet Plagiarism* (Senechal, 2000).
- *Plagiarism and Anti-Plagiarism* (Ehrlich, 1998).

CURRENT STATE OF INTERNET PAPER SITES

Term paper mills have been available on the Internet since 1996 and are international in scope. With names such as 'A-1 Termpapers', 'Essays International', 'Academic Termpapers', they might appear as benign sites. Some do provide basic research writing guidance but despite their rhetoric they are still paper mills. These sites are in the business of providing pre-written research papers. Most sites contain disclaimers telling potential buyers not to submit these papers for a grade, but students can and do turn in these papers as their own. Term paper mill sites come and go, but a list maintained at Coastal Carolina University (Kimbel Library, 2003) currently includes around 250 active term paper mill sites; when initiated in 1999, the list had just thirty-five such sites. The list was developed as a finding aid for local colleagues, to save time in tracking down possible sites and to provide a visual reminder of the widespread availability of term paper sites. The list is updated every six months.

The financial incentives for using Internet term paper mills can be very encouraging. Some sites give the papers away for free. Students simply cut and paste the paper to their computer or download a file. Other free sites give papers away, but students must register or turn in one of their papers to get a 'free' paper. Those that charge fees may do so as a membership fee or a per page charge ranging from US$1 to $10 a page. They will bill a credit card using a generic name such as 'Research Inc'. For students willing to pay a little extra, the paper can be emailed overnight so it can be turned in the next day. Custom papers are also available if the topic is too specialised for an off-the-shelf paper. These sites also run sales and summer 'special offers' to encourage use of the site.

What are students really getting with these papers? There is no guarantee of quality or currency. Many of the papers are several years old and are not reflective of current events or developments. The writing is largely mediocre and the research is minimal. In addition, many of the same 'free' papers are available at more than one site, leading to duplication and overuse. A frank discussion of the quality of custom papers was given several years ago by Witherspoon (1995) in her article for *Harper's Magazine*, 'This pen for hire . . . .' Witherspoon is a former writer of custom papers; she points out that she did it just for the money with little regard for content or quality, and the resulting papers reflected that motivation. They were up to the pass grade, but most certainly not in-depth.

In addition to the term 'paper mill sites', there are other options for the enterprising student. Many well-intentioned academics post their own papers and those of their really good students on personal or course web pages. Research sites include essay-length articles on topics of interest. Technical papers and conference proceedings are posted to disseminate information to professionals in the field. Students also attach papers or essays to their personal web pages. These types of sites do not have papers for sale and most include copyright warning statements.

However, an unscrupulous student may still copy and download a paper from these sites, change a few words or none at all and turn it in as their own work. Locating sites with these types of papers can be as easy as typing 'technical papers' on any Internet search engine.

DETECTING PLAGIARISED PAPERS

The following list of plagiarism signposts can help university teachers worldwide identify some of the common characteristics of plagiarised papers whether they are from the Internet or elsewhere.

1   The style, language or tone of the paper is not consistent. The flow of the paper is uneven or choppy, and sections may not relate to the previous ideas. The paper is written in a style above or below what the student usually turns in. It may not 'sound' like the student and odd phrases or expressions may be used. The spelling may be inconsistent with the country of origin, with 'American' spellings used in a paper turned in at a British university or English idioms in a paper turned in at an American university. But beware of criticism ahead of checking the student's computer spell-checker – since the software is generally of US origin it is very common for this to offer mis-corrections to students elsewhere in the world. Similar advice applies to use of the word processor's grammar-checker since usage varies from place to place and such software is generally not reliable. (But this is a matter for consideration by others!)

- Writing style, language, vocabulary, tone, grammar and so on is above or below that which the student usually produces.
- Idioms, language, and spelling are not native to the country and the student.
- Abrupt changes in style or vocabulary. Sentence tone and language change.
- Sections or sentences do not relate to the overall content of the paper. Students may 'personalise' a paper by adding a paragraph that ties the paper to the class assignment.

2   The physical appearance of the paper may be odd. Margins or formatting may be off. Numbering of pages, citations, footnotes, charts or graphs may not tally. There may be text cut off on the right-hand margin or sections of the paper may print with unusual symbols or text. The printed page may contain notations or web addresses that seem out of place. The physical appearance may contain shading or italics that do not belong logically on the page. Look out for:

- Strange text at the top or bottom of printed pages. These could be symbols, numbers or partial URLs.
- Grey letters in the text, often an indication that the page was downloaded from the Web, since colour letters on a screen tend to show up grey when printed in monochrome.
- Essays printed out from the student's web browser. These will typically have a URL at the top of the page and a date or time at the bottom of the page.
- Web addresses left at the top or bottom of the page. Many free essays have a tag line at the end of the essay that students often miss.
- Strange or poor layout. Papers that have been downloaded and reprinted often have page numbers, headings or spacing that just don't look right.

3   There are internal inconsistencies within the paper. The paper refers to additional materials that are not included in the paper. When asked to provide these accompanying materials, the student is unaware of their existence. The student is also unable to provide the requested items or re-create them. Works may be quoted in the text, but not included in the bibliography. Conversely, works cited in the footnotes or bibliography may not be used in the text. The paper may also refer to courses or individuals that are unfamiliar to the person reading the paper, which may indicate that the paper was previously used at another college or university. Look out for:

- References to graphs, charts, illustrations, figures or accompanying materials that are not there.
- References to footnotes that do not exist.
- References to classes that are not taught at your institution.

4   The citations are largely inaccurate or incorrect. They might cite materials that cannot be located in the institution's library and the student cannot provide proof that he or she requested the materials from another library through interlibrary loan. The works cited are all in another language or are primarily published in another country. The materials cited are in a language that the student neither speaks nor reads. Web citations refer to sites that are no longer active and the student cannot locate the new site because he or she does not know the name or substance of the original website. The publication dates of materials cited are all older than should be expected for the paper. Due to the age of the paper, there may be inaccurate references to events or historical figures, such as 'Prime Minister Thatcher said recently . . .'. From a UK perspective, the very construction 'Prime Minister Thatcher' would be suspect, as this sequence of words would not be expected of a British student.

When asked to provide additional information about their sources or to provide copies of cited material, students are unable to respond or locate the materials requested. Look out for:

- Citations to materials not owned by the university's library or which are all from another country or in a language unfamiliar to the student.
- Websites listed in citations are inactive. This can happen in non-plagiarised papers, but it is more common in older papers that are being reused.
- All citations are to materials that are older than five years.
- References are made to historical persons or events in the current tense.
- Students cannot identify citations or provide copies of the cited material.

5 Students cannot answer basic questions about the focus or content of the paper. When asked to write a summary paragraph, they are unable to recount the main ideas of the paper. Students who write their own papers will have a good sense of what they have already said.

- Students cannot summarise the main points of the paper.
- Students cannot answer questions about specific sections of the paper.

The appearance of more than one of these items should be an alert to look a little harder at the paper and the student's role in writing it. As librarians, the authors have seen several suspicious papers in the past few years that fell into at least one of these categories. In one instance, a student came in with a paper and asked for help in finding the required copies of the citations. The first clue was that two of the web pages cited had moved, and when the librarian found the new location of the pages, the student was unable to say if it was the right information, just that the author was the same. The second clue was when the third web page was located, the student cried out, 'But it's in German!' When asked if the page had been in German when it was originally cited, the student finally admitted that a room-mate wrote the paper for a class at another university. The student was advised to spend as much time writing a new paper as had already been spent on trying to pass off someone else's paper as their own. While this paper had not been purchased, it was still in the process of being plagiarised and was detected using the plagiarism signposts.

TRACKING DOWN PLAGIARISED PAPERS

University teachers may be able to locate the original paper on the Internet using a variety of techniques. The easiest is to identify a unique string of words in the paper. Using a variety of search engines, search for the phrase using quotes (' ') and the plus sign (+). For example, a paper on Jane Austen that uses the phrase 'fair share of monsters' in the first paragraph can be searched by typing in + 'Jane Austen' + 'fair share of monsters'. The website containing this essay is usually located in the first ten search results. Titles of papers may also be searched using quotes. If the student hasn't had the foresight to change the title, the paper title may be found on the index to a fee-based paper site. Students can also be asked to provide copies of selected sources cited in the paper; a student with a valid paper will be able to turn up most, if not all, of their sources.

Librarians are another source of assistance. A few minutes' consultation with a librarian may yield excellent results in identifying possible sources for a paper. Most university librarians are expert Internet researchers and knowledgeable about various sources or Internet sites that might assist in locating a plagiarised paper. Librarians can also help determine if specific citations exist or if the items are available locally.

With the rise in awareness of Internet-related plagiarism, several services have sprung up that offer plagiarism detection or verification services and software. Most of these services provide assistance for a fee either by single paper or by subscription. Sample sites include:

- Plagiarism.Org
- IntegriGuard
- Glatt Plagiarism Services, Inc.
- Essay Verification Engine
- WordChecksystems

Potential users are strongly advised to evaluate any such commercial service before using it, to take advantage of free trials and to read the fine print carefully.

UK universities and colleges have access to a publicly funded service based at the University of Northumbria (JISC, 2002) This was established to:

- provide generic advice on plagiarism
- offer students educational tools on plagiarism
- provide links to online resources
- give guidance on copyright and data protection issues

- link to an electronic plagiarism service
- offer training in the use of the above service.

Whether state-funded or commercial, these services can only be helpful in spotting duplicate phrases; it still requires a real person to determine if the duplication is a legitimate quotation or plagiarism.

COMBATING INTERNET PLAGIARISM

In most instances it is easier to combat plagiarism from the outset of the class than it is to deal with it later in the semester. Using term paper mills is a 'crime of opportunity'. Students faced with deadlines and a sense of being overwhelmed may turn to term paper mills. Students who have been guided in the research process and encouraged to think about the paper have less motive and less opportunity to turn in work that is not their own. University teachers may have to rethink the way they assign papers and research projects.

A checklist 'Seven easy steps to combat plagiarism' is given in Box 15.1. This outlines some basic techniques and issues that colleagues worldwide may use in any class to lessen the opportunities for plagiarism. Research papers or projects that are designed as an integral part of the course offer students a greater opportunity to learn. Well-thought-out assignments are less conducive to plagiarism. In addition, students learn quickly which teachers expect them to work and which don't!

BOX 15.1 SEVEN EASY STEPS TO COMBAT PLAGIARISM

1 Define what plagiarism is and is not.

- Make students aware of what constitutes plagiarism and how you handle it.
- Let students know that you know about term paper mills.
- Let students know that you check references and citations.
- Talk about copyright and the Internet.
- Talk about how to document web pages, how to document materials from online full text databases and the differences between web pages and online databases.
- Refer students to websites that discuss academic plagiarism. Examples include:

---

continued

Hinchliffe, L. (1998) *Cut-and-Paste Plagiarism: Preventing, Detecting, and Tracking Online Plagiarism* [online]. Available at: http://alexia.lis.uiuc.edu/~janicke/plagiary.htm.

Pearson, G. (1999) *Electronic Plagiarism Seminar* [online]. Available at: http://www.lemoyne.edu/library/plagiarism.htm.

2 Guide the research paper process. Don't let students get into a time crunch. Structure the research project so that it fulfils the goals of the class. Set up the project so that sections are worked on over the course of the semester.

3 Focus on the process of writing.

- Have different sections due at different times and provide feedback along the way. Provide written constructive criticism to let students know you really do read what they turn in.
- Have conferences with students regarding their progress and to see what they have produced so far.
- Being familiar with a student's style of writing, grammar and vocabulary makes it easier to determine if the student is the author of the paper.

4 Have students turn in any or all of the following over the course of a semester:

- A thesis statement/abstract.
- Written proposal for paper.
- Working or annotated bibliography.
- Rough draft or working notes.
- Outlines.
- All working drafts turned in with the final paper.
- Copies of cited references.

5 As part of the paper or as a separate assignment, have students reflect personally on the topic they are writing on or on the process of doing research and writing.

6 Make sure students know that you read all papers that are handed in, as it will enhance the final product.

7 Tie the topics into the class experience.

- Set writing assignments that encourage students to analyse classroom activities or discussions in light of the text.

- Use local issues as topics.
- Ask students to include a section in their term paper that discusses their topic in light of what was covered in class.
- In the final exam, ask students to summarise the main points of their research paper or project.

CONCLUSION

The 'Cheating: Paper Mills and You' workshop has been presented many times at Coastal Carolina University. In the workshops, teachers have been intensely interested in the subject, but had been reluctant to discuss plagiarism with their peers before the workshop. Some had been completely in the dark about the extent and ease of Internet plagiarism opportunities, while others had valuable advice to offer based on their experiences. Term paper mills are a fact of life and they are not going to go away as long as students feel they can get away with passing off another's work as their own. Educating teaching staff, librarians and students about plagiarism is the first step. The second step is to work with colleagues to address the problem and to develop effective preventive measures that minimise students' ability to turn in work that is not their own. With ongoing efforts, Internet paper mills can be countered.

REFERENCES

Ehrlich, H. (1998, revised and updated 2000) *Plagiarism and Anti-Plagiarism.* Available at http://newark.rutgers.edu/~ehrlich/plagiarism598.html (accessed February 2004).

Essay Verification Engine for Teachers. Available at http://www.canexus.com/eve/index.shtml (accessed February 2004).

Fain, M. and Bates, P. (1999, revised and updated 2003) *Cheating: Paper Mills and You.* Coastal Carolina University. Available at http://www.coastal.edu/library/papermil.htm (accessed February 2004).

Glatt Plagiarism Services, Inc. Available at http://plagiarism.com (accessed February 2004).

Harris, R. (2002) *Anti-Plagiarism Strategies for Research Papers.* Available at http://www.virtualsalt.com/antiplag.htm (accessed February 2004).

Hinchliffe, L. (1998) *Cut-and-Paste Plagiarism: Preventing, Detecting, and Tracking Online Plagiarism.* Available at http://alexia.lis.uiuc.edu/~janicke/plagiary.htm (accessed February 2004).

Joint Information Systems Committee (JISC) (2002) *Plagiarism Advisory Service.* Available at http://www.jiscpas.ac.uk (accessed February 2004).

Kimbel Library (2003) *Internet Paper Mills.* Available at http://www.coastal.edu/ library/mills2.htm (accessed February 2004).

Pearson, G. (1999) *Electronic Plagiarism Seminar.* Available at http://www.lemoyne. edu/library/plagiarism.htm (accessed February 2004).

Senechal, G. (2000) *Instructors Guide to Internet Plagiarism.* Available at http:// www.plagiarized.com/ (accessed February 2004).

Witherspoon, A. (1995) This pen for hire: on grinding out papers for college students. *Harper's Magazine,* June, pp. 49–58.

WordChecksystems. Available at http://www.wordchecksystems.com (accessed February 2004).

16

Developing a quality careers education using ICT

Arti Kumar

SUMMARY

Using ICT to deliver careers education is attracting considerable interest, especially in higher education institutions which can usually provide favourable conditions, such as easy access to the Internet. This chapter discusses some advantages and issues related to the introduction of career management skills online at the University of Reading and more recently at the University of Luton.

INTRODUCTION

Since 1999 the University of Reading's Careers Advisory Service has embarked on an ambitious project: the ultimate aim was to enable *all* their undergraduates to develop career management skills (CMS), thereby enhancing employability. This was to be achieved through a coherent, whole-institution approach, delivered through web-based materials supplemented by classroom-based tutorials, and included as part of their degree study in the penultimate year.

This chapter is based on the author's experience of helping to launch the CMS project while on secondment to the University of Reading. During this time the web-based educational materials were written up and piloted with two groups: 110 geography students and 60 chemistry students. A module handbook was written, with detailed assignment briefs and marking schemes, and staff development was undertaken.

An overview is provided of the rationale for the project. Before tackling the question 'Why deliver careers education through ICT?' there are more fundamental questions to be dealt with such as 'Why integrate careers education within the higher education curriculum?' and even 'What *is* careers education?' The content and aims of careers education are described in outline, with a view to assessing the relative advantages and disadvantages of delivering these through ICT. The pilots in the project have been evaluated and the key lessons learned have informed further developments. In conclusion, the current status is briefly explored in terms of achievements within Reading as well as the transferability of web-based CMS to other institutions.

THE INSTITUTION

The University of Reading is an established institution, reputed for the academic quality of its teaching and research. It is located on one main, pleasant campus – with two smaller sites nearby – about forty miles west of London. Its student population is approximately 12,500 (from all over the UK as well as overseas), of whom around 8,000 are undergraduates enrolled on an extensive range of academic and vocational subjects. It has good, comprehensive on-site IT facilities (400+ computers) and a linked local campus network, supported by technical services.

Far from resting complacently on its academic laurels, the University is concerned about developing students' employability and career management skills. For example, 'The Reading Graduate' is an innovative teaching and learning strategy which will embed key transferable skills and make them explicit within the curriculum, eventually providing a transcript to students identifying the distinctive qualities and attributes they should possess when they graduate. Another initiative in which the University is participating, Personal and Academic Records (PARs), aims to enhance students' personal tutorials and encourage them to reflect on the skills they are gaining, both within and outside of the curriculum.

THE CAREERS ADVISORY SERVICE (CAS)

The CAS is well resourced and staffed by a team of careers advisers who have expertise in guidance and groupwork skills, and a team of information staff who provide a range of career-related resources – paper-based, computer-based and videos – available in the careers library on the main campus. Their mission is '*to empower Reading graduates to successfully achieve their goals in the changing world of work and further learning*'.

They proactively attempt to achieve this mission in a variety of ways:

- Individual guidance interviews help with all aspects of career choice and job search.

- Vacancies notified by employers are regularly put on to a freely accessible database.
- A Job Shop advertises good-quality part-time work and vacation work for students.
- Two large careers fairs are run every year, with a wide range of employers attending.
- Regular employer presentations on campus are organised.
- A Work Experience Fair is organised, and CAS has appointed a Work Experience Officer.
- Careers advisers attempt to work with courses in various ways to develop a range of career-related skills (e.g. sessions on CV writing, interview skills, work placement briefing and debriefing).
- Careers staff offer a central 'Headstart' programme which consists of a series of workshops covering aspects of CMS, leading to credits for attendance and a University certificate.
- All the services mentioned above, as well as external careers events and opportunities, are publicised on the existing Careers Advisory Service web pages.

BACKGROUND AND RATIONALE FOR INTRODUCING INTEGRATED CMS

Historically, careers input within courses had to be continually negotiated with individual course tutors. Attendance at the workshops offered centrally by the Careers Advisory Service is optional. This has meant that students have been getting a sporadic and variable exposure to CMS at best. The majority of students postpone their career decision-making and planning until the final year, or even until after they have graduated. This can substantially delay their entry to a graduate-level position, as many vacancies for graduate schemes (and for postgraduate training) have early closing dates in the final year.

Integrating an accredited and assessed CMS module across the curriculum was felt to be a way of formalising collaborative relationships between the Careers Advisory Service and academic departments, and ensuring that all students would be better prepared for their transition into employment. At the same time, in common with other universities, Reading is having to contend with a number of pressures from various sources.

The government view

The UK government's 'competitiveness agenda' places a growing emphasis on the employability of graduates. All higher education institutions
are required to collect 'first destination statistics' to provide a picture
of what graduates do when they leave university. Official league tables
are produced each year by the Higher Education Statistics Agency, where
'employability' is one of the performance indicators by which universities
are judged (HESA, annual).

The Quality Assurance Agency (QAA) (2002a) has made several
recommendations that stress the importance of:

1   *'Integrating careers education, information and guidance within the
    curriculum for all higher education programmes of study.'*
2   *'Internal collaboration (between Careers Services and academic departments)
    as part of an institution-wide commitment to preparing students for their future
    careers.'*
3   Developing systems which enable students to build up progress files
    during their university experience, which will consist of a transcript
    of skills, and personal development planning (PDP), defined as *'a
    structured process undertaken by an individual to reflect upon their own
    learning, performance and/or achievement, and to plan for their personal,
    educational and career development'.*

The employer view

The Association of Graduate Recruiters (AGR) in its report *Skills for
Graduates in the 21st Century* (1995) described a range of key skills that
employers say the complete graduate needs. These include both ICT skills
and 'self-reliance' – the ability to manage their career and personal
development.

Many employers are using the Internet not only to market themselves
but as a recruitment tool. For example, an AGR report (2000) which
focused on fifty-six major employers in ten European countries found
that the number of employers using the Internet grew from 15 per cent
to 91 per cent between 1996 and 1999. Fifty-nine per cent of the
employers surveyed allowed graduates to submit online applications,
although many said they found it hard to attract graduates who possessed
the skills they wanted.

The student view

The government subsidises higher education less and less each year. A
new fee structure has been imposed which places more of a financial

burden on students and their parents. Within this new fees environment it is likely that prospective students will give substantial consideration to employment opportunities after graduation when choosing their degree courses and institutions. Students are usually all too aware that:

- The contemporary world of work is subject to rapid change, technological advance, increasing globalisation and sophisticated consumer demand.
- The whole area of career choice has become more open-ended, complex, diverse and competitive.
- Increasing numbers of graduates will be chasing fewer 'graduate jobs'.
- Entry to graduate-level positions is usually through a demanding selection process, and job search skills are increasingly important.
- Career choice and career development do not involve a once-only decision – students will need to be prepared to keep re-evaluating and making career decisions throughout future careers of constant change and continuous learning.

Despite students' awareness of labour market conditions, experience, research and evaluation in universities has shown that most undergraduates will not or cannot make time to incorporate career planning into a busy lifestyle (many have part-time jobs on the side while studying) unless it is an accredited and compulsory part of the curriculum.

The university response

Traditionally, the belief held was that possession of a degree was an automatic passport to a career. Today universities feel compelled to respond to the external pressures outlined above, and most are attempting to deal with the changed situation by including skills development within the curriculum, and making such incentives explicit to students. Many also offer some form of work-related and/or career-related education.

For all these reasons, the University of Reading has formulated policies and implemented strategies to remain competitive in the area of 'employability'. More recently, the University Strategy for Teaching and Learning specified both ICT and CMS as skill areas (among others) to be developed by all students, and allocated resources to enable CMS to be integrated into all undergraduate courses as a matter of urgency.

WHAT IS CMS, AND HOW CAN IT HELP?

Careers education, where it occurs in the higher education curriculum, is variously entitled career management/planning skills, career development learning or career capability. Despite some variation in content, all such units or modules are based on a commonly accepted generic model, capable of adaptation to level and subject area. It may be defined as *'a formal process owned by the individual to develop skills and knowledge for managing and implementing future personal and career change'*.

At Reading, 'CMS online' was developed as a web-based package containing three essential CMS building blocks, with three assignments attached to each block. These three elements are closely interrelated, and build up sequentially:

1   Realistic self-assessment in 'Finding Your Profile' gives students a clearer sense of vocational self and direction.
2   Career exploration and an analytical job study in 'Finding the Fit' enables students to identify and retrieve information of relevance to them, generate ideas, understand the labour market and its demands, assess different options available to them, and use their profile as a yardstick to target *suitable* jobs/organisations/other options.
3   'Effective Applications' brings together two propositional areas of knowledge: 'self-knowledge' from (1) matched with 'job knowledge' from (2). In the CMS equation, these add up to the ability to justify and promote one's career choices and cope effectively with graduate recruitment.

The process is generic and applies to all students, regardless of their degree discipline, and regardless of whether the individual wants to be a doctor or a 'dotcommer'. The information required will accordingly be different, but CMS online has the potential for customisation to particular subject and occupational fields through guided access to specific information. (This potential has since been further exploited in the development of the package, acting upon evaluation by staff and students. 'Finding the Fit' allows students to enter that section by choosing their particular degree subject – which then takes them to selected research resources relevant to their specific needs.)

ADVANTAGES OF USING ICT TO DELIVER CMS

What can be gained, and what must be sacrificed by delivering CMS online? Those who have used mainly face-to-face contact, student-centred and activity-driven methods in the classroom to develop CMS are often most sceptical about using ICT as a delivery mechanism. However, given that limited resources and increased student numbers do not always allow many hours of direct contact in the current climate of higher education, ICT must in effect be considered a saving grace.

The first point to emphasise here is that ICT may be used in addition to rather than as a substitute for other methods. At Reading the CMS module consists of three two-hour tutorials in the classroom, each scheduled to precede and launch the three sections of CMS online. In addition, the range of career-related services provided at Reading (listed above: see 'The Careers Advisory Service') is still available to supplement CMS. The focus of evaluation should not only be on the technology but on the complex activity and learning it is meant to support. Before we go on to assess the part played by ICT in the CMS learning process, let us look at some fairly general advantages of using it.

Efficiency gains

- Careers materials date quite rapidly, and it is easier to update online material than books which are in print.
- One is not constrained by cost and space related to numbers of printed pages.
- It reduces the need to maintain stocks of hard copy.
- Users can download and print just what they need when they need it.
- This represents a considerable saving in printing and reprographics costs for the providers – and there should be benefits in terms of environmental conservation as there is less waste of paper, printing ink and services' resources.
- It is relatively easy to tap into a range of external sources for research and information, and it is easy to cross-reference to other sources.
- The CMS resource may also be used as a stand-alone package for independent learning – at different stages and levels – for information only, or for guidance and educational purposes.
- It allows for flexible, self-managed information retrieval and learning: a large volume of material is available for the Careers Advisory Service, academic staff and students to access remotely and independently.

Widening access and equality of opportunity

Physical access
Some of the points mentioned above relate to providing a resource with universal access and availability. Technology has been increasingly absorbed into the higher education culture, and it is now the norm for

students to word-process their essays, and to use the Internet and email. Physical access to computers and back-up services at Reading is not an issue as there are sufficient machines available over long hours for drop-in use, with free and easy access to the Internet. For those incoming students who need training in ICT there are workshops, guides, self-teach materials, online help and support staff.

Relying totally or heavily on web-based materials can of course exacerbate inequalities for people with certain disabilities, especially visual impairment. At Reading one of the careers advisers had to have this special need taken into account, but technical methods to overcome such barriers were used. Multi-mode alternatives such as audio or hard copies of the text would otherwise provide access for those students to whom the Internet is not available, or where a disability precludes access.

Access to information

The Internet already holds a wealth of career-related information: there are literally hundreds of sites which contribute in one way or another to CMS. Researching these, it was found that the vast majority contain elements of CMS – either self-assessment questionnaires, psychometrics online, information about occupations, employers and vacancies, CV and interview advice – a piecemeal approach. It therefore made sense for Reading's CMS module to adopt as holistic an approach as possible, integrating the entire process and making it explicit for students in a structured, comprehensive manner.

In order to achieve this, the CMS site had to contain a great deal of tutorial material in itself, but also act as a gateway to relevant external sites. Learning about 'careers' can include just about everything under the sun – amounting to sheer information overload! Students cast adrift on these uncharted seas of career-related information are more likely to drown than to 'surf the web'. An important part of the task was therefore to give them a life-jacket – guided, structured access to appropriate information – by creating selected links and explaining why they might use them, at the right time, in the sequential process of learning.

Initially, web links were scattered through each section: they were well signposted and explained, and allowed students personalised navigation through the maze. In effect this is similar to giving a book reader further references, but the difference is that a web user can enter other sites at one click of the mouse – and yet other sites through that site – so the potential for creating an information maze and losing people within it is great. In developing the package, therefore, a more linear, workbook approach has now been adopted, and most of the web links are offered at the end of each section, so the temptation to browse and wander off track is minimised. Students now consistently rate ease of navigation in CMS online highly.

A technical feature in the CMS package is that it does not only link students to recommended sites but takes them directly to the relevant page. In addition, they can 'retrace their steps' back to their original place in the CMS package by simply clicking on to the cross at the top of the page, without having to constantly use the 'back' button – no matter how far they have travelled into the external site.

Access to learning

There is plenty of evidence from observation and research that the younger generation today is quick and efficient at handling information, but the real challenge for educators is to assess what and how much may be learned through ICT. Perhaps the difference between simply knowing something and understanding it critically is in the analytical depth and scope of learning. Importantly, in the case of CMS, that learning needs to be applicable to an individual's situation, and lead to sustainable action.

If it is to enhance immediate and future employability, it must give people the skills and knowledge to get a job of their choice now (at a graduate level), survive and thrive in the job, and change jobs in the future. It must provide the foundation for lifelong learning. Viewed from this dynamic angle, CMS online takes on an added significance. The module is offered during their penultimate year to encourage students to plan ahead, make timely decisions and meet early application deadlines. However, having the resource online means it can be returned to in their final year or even after they have graduated – whenever they actually apply for jobs and attend selection centres and interviews.

An essential injunction in CMS is to remember that the process is cyclical and continuous. For example, the attributes defined in 'Finding Your Profile' are not static – skills can be developed, values can change. Given that both 'self' and 'jobs' are subject to continuous change and development, review is an important part of the process. The three interrelated components of CMS may in themselves result in further learning, review and adjustment – taking the process far beyond the boundaries of the CMS module, into the future.

CMS online gives students the tools they need to discover the things they need to know, putting them in control of the material. The importance of each section within the process of building up CMS is explained, with built-in analytical questions to encourage reflection and probe beneath the surface. Tutorials were further used to enthuse students to engage with the material appropriately.

The module was piloted with a large group – 110 geography students – but even so, lecture input was interspersed with interactive opportunities for students to divide into smaller groups for discussion, and to practise and develop skills, for example, role-playing a selection interview. In fact, one could say that having CMS online liberated contact time in the classroom to be devoted to group activity, analysis and interpretation of information rather than simply giving information. Evaluation indicated that this variety of learning methods was highly valued by students. Having web-based material also helps to accommodate the learning style of students who prefer reading, reflection and more time to absorb concepts.

The *Module Handbook* and all course details (contacts, assignment briefs, marking criteria and grading schemes) were all put online for ease of reference, but were also given out as hard copies and explained during tutorials. The importance of the assignments in encouraging analytical, deep learning cannot be emphasised too much. For example, the first assignment on 'Finding Your Profile' required students to rate their abilities and aptitudes, prioritise career values and interests, and identify personality traits in relation to specific occupations – in very interactive and reflective ways.

Students may use the questionnaires within the CMS website, and also link to other sites, but the mix of constructivist and psychometric models they are required to use is intended to elicit in-depth and systematic self-assessment. The aim is to clarify different facets of the 'vocational self-concept' from a variety of angles, using a range of techniques. The assignment then requires them to consider the synergy from any patterns emerging, and also to take into account their personal career history and circumstances.

The potential tendency to be simplistic and reductionist in such a venture had to be countered by injunctions in the assignment brief, to the effect that reliance on the results of psychometric instruments must be tempered by evidence from real life and feedback from other people. Students therefore had to find real-life examples to demonstrate the attributes they claimed, just as they would have to when defending their choice of job and organisation during graduate recruitment procedures – whether in CVs, covering letters and applications forms, or at interviews.

Learning features in 'Finding the Fit' include:

- guided access to relevant external sites connected with all the options available to graduates (e.g. employment, postgraduate study, time out opportunities, temporary work abroad);
- advice and questions to ask when considering and researching such opportunities;

- understanding the graduate labour market;
- guidelines on evaluating a range of information sources and using them effectively, including the Internet;
- investigating a job analytically, and ground rules for finding and interviewing someone doing that job;
- investigating an organisation and sector in which that job occurs;
- guidelines on writing a report;
- becoming aware of and selectively using a variety of job search methods and sources of vacancy information, including the Internet as an emerging major tool in graduate recruitment.

Similarly, the third section, 'Effective Applications', has interactive exercises that help students interpret and engage with the recruitment process, to understand why employers ask certain questions, and the criteria they then use to assess an applicant's response. This section particularly fosters lateral thinking: the making of connections between self, jobs, employer criteria and selection procedures. It also develops self-promotion skills: the type of concise and selective writing skills needed for effective CVs and covering letters, and verbal and social skills for coping with interviews. Such skills may therefore be developed to some extent from using the web-based CMS package alone, but are further reinforced by and practised in the classroom-based tutorials.

Access to social interaction and contacts

The opponents of online learning often worry that this new technology will create a nation of reclusives who are unable to interact with others. It is true that much of the CMS material requires individual solitary engagement, but the importance of social, interpersonal and networking skills for employability is emphasised and explained online, and team work is practised in the tutorials. Not only does the module encourage students to experience the world of work, it also gives them access to the external world through a list of potential contacts on the alumni database, links to professional associations and employers. In undertaking the 'Job Study' assignment, they are given guidelines for informational interviewing and encouraged to go out and interview someone doing a job in which they are interested.

Communication via email links is also possible, and several career-related sites include the opportunity to post queries on bulletin boards or join discussion groups. This method of communication may be preferred by some, and could actually boost the confidence of introverted students. Email links to key members of staff within 'CMS online' give students the opportunity to make suggestions for improvements and modifications to the module, to point out technical problems and request help.

INTEGRATING THE PROVISION OF CAREERS EDUCATION, INFORMATION AND GUIDANCE

One of the recommendations of the Quality Assurance Agency (see 'The government view' above) is that this area of provision should be integrated into the curriculum, through closer collaboration between the careers service and academic departments. CMS online gives both students and staff access to the full range of career-related services and events through the tutorial material, as these are referred to and 'marketed' at key points. For example, the significance of individual guidance, employer presentations and CV workshops is made explicit in the process of career development learning, so students are more likely to make more of such optional face-to-face provision as well.

Having the web-based module also creates a setting in which students and staff own a body of shared knowledge, concepts and metaphors related to CMS. It facilitates the collaborative endeavour. It meets exactly the QAA requirement (2002b) for all students in higher education – that they develop progress files which contain a transcript of 'Skills and Personal Development Planning'.

LESSONS LEARNED AND TRANSFERABILITY OF THE MODEL

The author has transferred some of the benefits gained from her experience at Reading to her home institution, the University of Luton. The model developed at Reading is highly relevant to students taking the Career Development Module, currently in its seventh year at Luton, which the author coordinates. However, since the Luton module is at Level 2 bearing fifteen credits, it includes substantial staff–student contact via twelve workshop-style classroom sessions. The web material is referred to, and the skills-oriented, interactive exercises are required as set 'homework topics', which are then discussed in class. It has also been appropriate to add more specific academic material – for example, on the theories of career choice and decision-making, and more information on the graduate labour market. Text-intensive files may be downloaded and printed, so that students are not expected to read large volumes of text on screen.

For the advantages of online learning to be realised and maintained, certain conditions need to prevail. These include:

- **Motivating students**: Evaluation of CMS online has shown that most students are perfectly comfortable with using the Web and learning from it. For those who are not, additional support needs to be provided. However, most students produced assignments to a high standard from the material given. Engaging with CMS requires self-discipline and motivation – and it is evident from the pilots that nothing motivates students better than giving them clear assignment briefs and academic credits for the work involved.
- **Staff development**: Academic staff involved in the delivery at Reading are invited to sessions which introduce CMS content, aims and concepts, including the online material. They also observe the tutorials delivered initially by careers advisers. For staff to take over the design, delivery and assessment of CMS eventually, it is imperative that they become thoroughly familiar with the material and subscribe to the underpinning philosophy. Opportunities to review sessions jointly and plan ahead are important.

   All this is often difficult in universities due to pressure on academic staff to teach, research and undertake administrative functions. Such pressures often leave little or no time to invest in learning new skills. Innovative methods in teaching and learning rarely achieve the priority they deserve due to the lack of recognition at an institutional and national level for such innovation. Recognising such constraints, the Implementation Task Group at Reading recommended that more recently 'a partnership approach be adopted' between CAS and academic staff – thereby developing closer links and pooling the best strengths of both parties.
- **Technical expertise** is required both in writing the text and converting it to 'chunks and layers' appropriate for the non-linear manner in which the web presents information. The material must grab students and retain them, or encourage them to return (CMS assignments helped in this respect!). To present comprehensive material yet allow selective use, devices such as pop-up boxes were used, as well as hyperlinked text and access to external sites. Giving the user control is important, through guided access and navigation.

   Technical competence is also required by careers advisers and other staff involved in demonstrating CMS online to students, and using the related PowerPoint presentations. Such training is offered, but some staff take to this more readily than others.
- **Content management and updating**: If quality of content is to be maintained as regards the currency, accuracy and reliability of

information, then keeping a watching brief on the site is essential. Students were involved in facilitating maintenance: a message was incorporated on the site asking them to email the 'webmaster' to alert him to any links or technical aspects that did not work.

The scope for development in meeting the needs of specific subject departments is being addressed. For example, relevant new web-links are now being continually assessed and included, in order to tailor the material more to subject areas and occupations as the project is rolled out to bring them on board. Careers information staff lead and initiate in doing this, then involve careers advisers and subject staff – so that there is eventually team involvement and ownership of the material.

- **Potential for multimedia development**: There is scope for the use of multimedia, but adding audio and/or video clips to the CMS package must be weighed against its fitness for purpose. Decisions always need to be made about whether and how one wishes to interest and entertain in educating, and what impressions one wishes to convey.

CONCLUSION

CMS using ICT can claim to improve on the previous situation in many ways. It is certainly consistent with all the recommendations and policies outlined in the 'Rationale' section above. Since its inception early in 2000, the project has proceeded successfully by and large, achieving its aims by enabling more and more undergraduates to enhance their personal and professional development skills as part of the curriculum. CMS online is playing an essential part in that success, and will continue to evolve. Feedback has continually indicated that students are not passive recipients of CMS information, but active participants in personalised career development learning.

An increasing number of academic staff have been 'converted', and most departments are now involved in delivering and assessing careers education. The project has provided a quality framework and strategy for the delivery of institution-wide CMS, thereby establishing the expertise of the Careers Advisory Service, and promoting its role in supporting academic staff.

Following a number of presentations and favourable reviews, enquiries were received from several other institutions that were introducing or developing careers education programmes (including some overseas). Reading decided to make CMS online available to them at a reasonable cost. From Reading's success in selling the package it seems obvious that the underpinning model is very transferable across the higher education sector, and flexible enough to be adapted relatively easily to other institutions' specific needs. Access to the package is now restricted by special password, but sample pages are available online (University of Reading, undated).

REFERENCES

Association of Graduate Recruiters (AGR) (1995) *Skills for Graduates in the 21st Century*, Cambridge: Association of Graduate Recruiters.

Association of Graduate Recruiters (AGR) (2000) *Fourth European Recruiters' Report*, summarised in AGR Newsletter *Janus*, June.

Higher Education Statistics Agency (HESA) (annual) *First Destinations of Students Leaving HEIs*, Cheltenham: HESA Services Ltd. Available at http://www.hesa. ac.uk/ (accessed March 2003).

Quality Assurance Agency (QAA) (2002a) *Code of Practice for the Assurance of Academic Quality and Standards in Higher Education (Section 8 – Careers Education, Information and Guidance)*, Cheltenham: QAA. Available at http://www.qaa.ac. uk/public/cop/codesofpractice.htm (accessed March 2003).

Quality Assurance Agency (QAA) (2002b) *Developing a Progress File for Higher Education: Summary Report of the Consultation Exercise*, Cheltenham: QAA. Available at http://www.qaa.ac.uk/crntwork/progfilehe/contents.htm (accessed March 2003).

University of Reading (undated) *Career Management Skills Online Demonstration Materials*. Available at http://www.rdg.ac.uk/careers/cmsdemo/ (accessed March 2003).

Watts, A.G., Law, B., Killeen, J., Kidd, J.M. and Hawthorn, R. (1996) *Rethinking Careers Education and Guidance: Theory, Policy and Practice*, London: Routledge.

Index

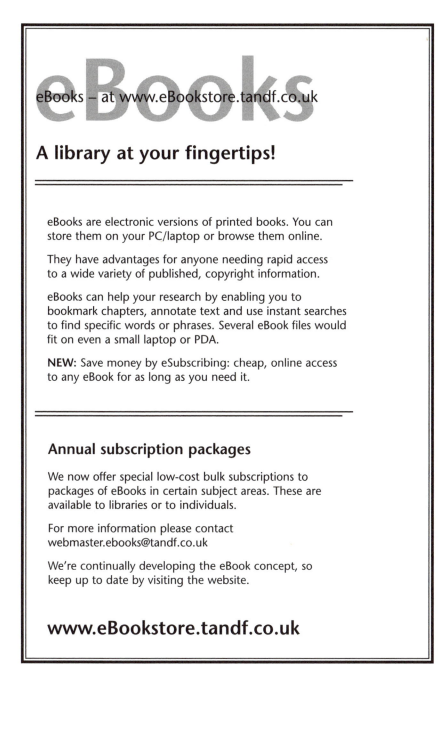